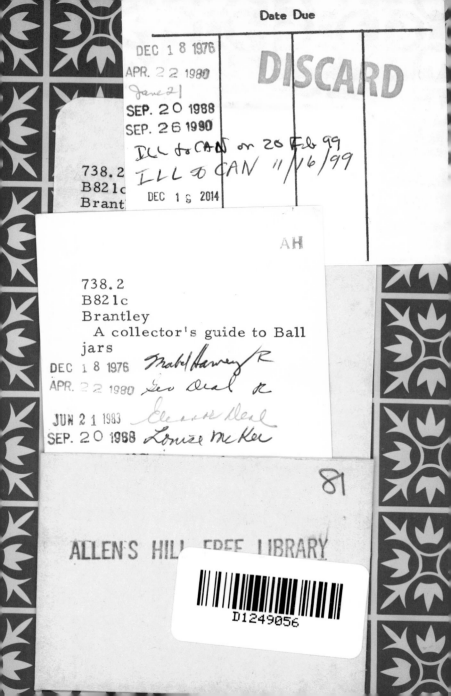

To the millions of home canners who
have made fruit jar collecting
possible.
To my mother, Frances Chappell Brantley,
the first home canner I ever knew.
And to my wife, Peggy Stebbins
Brantley, the best home canner
I know.

A Collector's Guide to

BALL JARS

By William F. Brantley

Foreword by Edmund F. Ball
Color Photography by David A. Harris

Muncie, Indiana
Rosemary Humbert Martin *Publisher*
1975

TABLE OF CONTENTS

This neon advertising sign for Ball Jars
was discovered several years ago in a
vacant warehouse at Ball's Muncie
facility. It apparently dates from just
before World War II and ones like it
were used in groceries over Ball
jar displays or in store windows to tell
homemakers that the merchant
carried America's best-known brand of
food preserving supplies.

OVERLEAF *(Plate 1.)*
In the nearly two centuries since the founding of the American
republic, mankind has found ways of accomplishing two
significant achievements — providing an abundance of food and
reaching the moon. This photograph of two singular Ball achievements —
fruit jars and a satellite, a model of the Orbiting Solar Observatory,
of which Ball built seven — shows the development
of the company over 95 years. The American Flag,
symbolizing the bounty and goodness of our nation and
its willingness to help men of good will everywhere,
and the bust of our first President and the commemorative medal
of our current President, show the range of republican history.
The ticker tape is from the morning Ball stock was admitted to
trading on the New York Stock Exchange, December 17, 1973.
The pickles were canned in 1974 by the author's wife and are
San Marzano tomatoes. The Bicentennial jar will be sold in 1975.
The mug is a commemorative of Neil Armstrong's walk on the moon
in 1969, showing the front page of the Findlay, Ohio, Republican-Courier,
edited by Edwin Hemminger. Findlay is a city important in Ball history.
The coverlet, of wool — grown, sheared, carded, spun, dyed and
woven by hand — is from the author's aunt, Margaret Brantley Cone Cable.
It was made in the early 1800s in Nash County, N. C., by her
grandmother's sister. The brown in the coverlet is hickory-bark dyed,
fixed with copper pennies. The cream is natural wool and the blue
is from indigo. Flax to sew the coverlet was grown on the
family farm and spun into thread. The traditional virtues of
self-reliance, pride in the nation, and patriotism are expressed
in this photograph of fruit jars and satellites.

FOREWORD

With a resurging interest in the home preservation of foods and the elevation of the earlier types of fruit jars to prize collectors' items, a book on the subject of home canning jars — and particularly Ball jars — is most timely.

The history of food preservation is really the history of civilization. Man rose above the lesser animals when over eons and through painful trial and error he learned to harvest and preserve his supplies of food. The art of drying, smoking and salting meat and storing vegetables and grain was passed on to succeeding generations, each adding its improved techniques. Procurement and protection of supplies of food led to the formation of families, tribes, and clans. Eventually settlements were created from which towns and cities emerged. Nations grew basically around common resources and the availability of adequate supplies of food. Battles were fought, wars won or lost, nations rose and fell for lack of food — even entire civilizations disappeared.

It was not until the nineteenth century that a most unlikely triumvirate developed the processes that made possible the convenient preservation and packaging of food. One was a self-proclaimed emperor, another an obscure French confectionist, and the third a querulous, cantankerous tinsmith from Brooklyn, New York. The emperor was Napoleon Bonaparte who offered a prize of 12,000 francs to the person discovering a means to provide nourishing food for his scurvy-plagued armies. The confectionist was a Parisian named Nicholas Appert who won Napoleon's prize through his publication in 1810 of principles for food preservation by sterilization. The tinsmith was John Landis Mason, who in 1858 designed and patented a screw finish for a glass jar with a shoulder on which a screw closure and gasket could easily and reliably form an hermetic seal.

Shortly over a decade after the terrible War Between the States, the five young Ball brothers moved off a farm in upper New York State and purchased with $200 borrowed from a preacher-uncle a small business located in Buffalo manufacturing wood-jacketed cans for shipping oils and varnishes. Always alert to changing times and attractive opportunities, they soon took on the assembling of tin-jacketed glass containers used for holding kerosene for fueling lamps used in every home in those days before electricity. Shortly, a group of Belgian glass blowers, drifting southward from Canada, convinced them that they could manufacture their own glass containers. With surplus capacity, they sought other glass products to manufacture. John Mason's 1858 patent had long since expired, but they recognized the practical features of his design and began the manufacturing of the "Ball Mason Fruit Jar" which, for almost a century now, has been a household word.

After their little factory in Buffalo was destroyed by fire in 1886, they decided to move to the Middle West seeking cheaper

(Plate 2.) The first Ball Brothers glass plant, in 1887, before it was completed in 1888 in Muncie. The office is the building in the foreground at right. Workmen can be seen on the roof, left center.

fuel to operate their glass furnaces and to be closer to the fast-growing, western markets. Muncie, Indiana, where they eventually decided to locate, was a little community then of some 6,000 people of which they had never previously heard. Responding to a telegram from a "Citizens Committee," the young president, Frank C. Ball, visited the town and records in his "Memoirs" that, "Here the men were all courteous, kind, and businesslike." Here they moved, made their lifelong homes, raised their families, and developed an industry that now is worldwide and literally produces products ranging: "From Fruit Jars to Satellites."

The story of the fruit jar can be correlated with the past century of our country's history. It has played a significant role through pioneer days, depressions, droughts, shortages, wars, good times and bad. Home canners have led the way in developing balanced diets of wholesome, nutritious foods from which economical meals to suit all tastes and special dietary needs can be produced.

"A Collector's Guide to Ball Jars" will be an informative and interesting guidebook for collectors. Students of the social sciences, economists and historians will find it to be an excellent source of materials for research and studies. It will be equally informative and interesting as well as just plain good reading for the average person who may be interested in the story of a simple, commonplace, household item that has played an important role in the development of our country and from which has grown a successful, worldwide enterprise.

EDMUND F. BALL
Muncie, Indiana
January 8, 1975

(Plate 3.) Ball President Frank C. Ball reads papers at his desk at the Muncie plant in this photograph taken in March 1903. A photograph of four of his children hangs over the desk, along with a calendar from the Ottawa Sand Company, Ottawa, Illinois.

OVERLEAF AND COVER *(Plate 4.)*
Ball began producing tin-jacketed glass kerosene jugs in the early
1800s for convenient, safe transport of fuel oil to homes
which were using oil lamps. In 1885 the young brothers
turned to making fruit jars like the "Buffalo" jar at left.
In 1895 they made the wire bail jar, center right,
and then the 3-L Ball Mason, which is filled with pears canned in 1903.
About the time the young brothers were beginning their
jar enterprise, seven young sisters named Wright made this quilt
in their western Kentucky home, embroidering their names and
those of their five brothers on the patchwork.
One of the seven girls was the author's grandmother, Martha.
She and her sister Addie attended the 1904 World's Fair in St. Louis
where they purchased the cranberry glass.
Here it sets on a riverfront levee stone from St. Louis.
The milk glass lamp was given the author's mother by a
neighbor many years ago in North Carolina.
The background barn siding is from a venerable Hoosier farm
structure now owned by Mr. and Mrs. Paul Boltz of Albany, Indiana.

PREFACE

A few months ago, Miss Jan Rose, a former colleague of mine in St. Louis, suggested: "You should write a collector's guide to Ball jars." She had been cleaning out the accumulation of family treasures which had been flooded by the Mississippi River in the spring of 1973 and had found fruit jars among items left by her grandmother and her father.

I did not then realize she had given me the title for this book. But her request was only the first of hundreds I received for some guide to fruit jars made by Ball over the past 90 years.

The book has come together through the cooperation of many friends and associates. My greatest debt is to Dick Roller of Paris, Illinois, the man I consider to be America's premier fruit jar expert.

Props for some of the photographs came not only from my family's collection but also from the antique collections of Mrs. Audrey Boltz of Albany, Indiana, and Mrs. Judy Keck of Muncie, Indiana, from the Delaware County Cooperative Extension Service in Muncie, and through the assistance of Max Buell of Muncie.

Jars came from the Ball Corporation Museum and from the collections of Dick and Jennie Roller, and Dennis Orosz, Ronald Mixell, Richard Cole, Joe Kozlowski, Irma Brown, Norman and Junne Barnett and the author's personal collection. Dick's collection yielded the Ball box ends and old advertising matter, and the unusual letter openers belong to Vern C. Schranz and Norman Barnett.

Preparation of the jars — the washing and polishing before photography — was done by my generous colleagues who gave their time before and after their usual working hours. Sorting, washing, rinsing, second rinsing and drying were accomplished by Dennis Orosz, Gary South, Brenda Stone, Irma Brown, and Pauline Williams.

Dennis Orosz rendered invaluable assistance in copying old pictures and advertisements and in photostating historic documents, autographs and trademarks, devoting dozens of evening and weekend hours for which I am deeply indebted and grateful.

Deep appreciation is due and given to Miss Elisabeth Ball, Mrs. Margaret Ball Petty, Alexander M. Bracken, and Edmund F. Ball for gracious sharing of memories.

Others of my colleagues who rendered invaluable contributions of information and/or encouragement were John Fisher, Dick Ringoen, Vern Schranz, Stan Stuart, George Loughery, Howard Jones, Russ Simpson, Elmer Cox, Johnnie Ketchem and Norm Rappe.

I am also indebted to Arleta Rodrigues, Russ Willis, Dick Roller and Norman Barnett, all advanced jar collectors, who read the manuscript and offered suggestions.

Jack Kemper Carmichael, friend and colleague, also read the work with his eagle-sharp eye for grammar and spelling errors.

Two women, however, have been the most help — Rosemary Martin, my longtime friend and now my publisher, and her friend since they were first-graders together, my wife, Peggy. Without Rosemary's consistent good humor and wise guidance and without the forebearance of my wife, this could not have been accomplished.

The book is incomplete. However, it does contain some previously unreported jars. A scant 15 years ago there were perhaps a dozen serious collectors in America. Today fruit jar collectors are estimated to number somewhere between 40,000 and 100,000. Many of their collections contain several hundred jars. A few are specialized in Ball only, or pints only, or pre-1900 jars only, or post-World War II jars, or certain colors only.

Fruit jar collectors are no different from other collectors. They are enterprising individuals who have found something beautiful, reasonably inexpensive (although some jars command prices of $500 and more), and something different.

Those I know like fruit jars because they have a sense of history — their penchant for tracing industrial history is highly developed, or they have a sociological sense of how Americans have raised their standards of living by having better and more plentiful food, or they have an aesthetic sense which makes them appreciate the intrinsic beauty of glass in a variety of colors and shapes. Others merely may be pack rats with some organizational ability.

Collectors are not uncommon in America. I believe collecting today is a method or form we have developed to give ourselves a sense of belonging to a place and a time — a sense continually assaulted by the pressures of modern and transitory life.

To those who have their collections of thimbles, gems, coins, stamps, antique automobiles, weeds, plates, bottles, coffee cans, dictionaries, Bibles, magazine covers, National Geographics, barbed wire, beer cans, eyeglasses, Oriental rugs, patchwork quilts, farm implements and on and on, I salute them with affection. However, make mine fruit jars, especially Ball fruit jars.

No company has made fruit jars as long as Ball. No company has made so many fruit jars or so many different kinds. And I believe no company has contributed so richly to the good life we live today through its food preservation activities as Ball.

I have tried to avoid all of the "errors" in Ball jars — the ones with slight mistakes. There are simply too many. Mold makers made mistakes as we all do. Their mistakes can make interesting collections by themselves. I consider these jars no more or less valuable than the "correct" versions.

No attempt has been made to price any of the jars. That's for the marketplace — the free enterprise system. There are two or three fine price guides which I can recommend and which I use. These are good reference works and will be found in the back of the book along with other references.

Color fidelity has been sought — this being the first book on fruit jars to picture the jars in color throughout. There are numerous colors in Ball jars — the aqua (a blue-green) which is found in many jars, amber in several shades, green in several shades, flint (the clear) which sometimes has turned a smoky gray or a lavender or pink or honey amber by the sun, and Ball blue, a rich, distinctive blue which Ball developed and controlled with amazing consistency for some 40 years. This Ball blue is known to collectors around the world and is probably the most distinctive color in jars. In many instances, in jars which were made for special orders, the presence of the Ball blue color is a sure way of determining that they were made by Ball. Part of the reason for this color was due to sand from Lake Michigan's southeastern shore area which was used by Ball.

Efforts will be made in anticipated subsequent editions to correct inaccuracies and to report any new finds of older jars as well as to report newer Ball jars. You will find the jars for 1975 in this book — the Bicentennial reissue of Ball Ideal as well as the Ball Mason with the metric marks on the side opposite the traditional cups and ounces marks.

My earliest recollection of Ball jars is from about the age of three in North Carolina when peaches came from one on a cold winter morning, canned by my mother, my aunt or my grandmother. My first remembrance of canning was picking tomatoes for canning on D-Day in 1944. And my first Ball jar which I kept was given me by a young nurse at Ball Memorial Hospital which contained my gallstones — 59 of them in 1959. That young nurse is now my wife. Forgive me as I tell you that the complications of my surgery included not only a wife and three sons, but an addiction to Ball jars.

BILL BRANTLEY
Selma, Indiana
December 7, 1974

Plate 5

(Plate 6.)
Put Muncie on TOP Save Every Good . . .
The wooden box ends, now antique "go-withs,"
show Ball's early involvement in packaging,
offering a dozen jars to the consumer in a single package, beginning in 1894.
The small "The Ball Jar," center,
is one of the very first made in Muncie in 1888.
The flint quart "Perfect Mason" at the left
is the last jar ever made in Muncie, on March 19, 1962,
as the label indicates.
It was made from Tank 2, Machine 1.
The antique scoop contains "batch" — lime, sand and soda ash —
from the old Muncie batchhouse.
The foreground bricks are from abandoned sidings of part of the
Muncie & Western Railroad, as are the spike and rail leveler.
The yellow bricks are fire bricks from the Muncie furnace after it was dis-
mantled. The weekly time book was found in an abandoned warehouse.
The pencil clip is another "go-with."
The 74 years of Ball glassmaking in Muncie are summed up here.

I

From the Beginning

In 1960, Edmund F. Ball, then chairman of the board and president of Ball Brothers Company, Inc., addressed the Chicago dinner of The Newcomen Society in North America. Mr. Ball's address, coming at the beginning of the great American effort to put man on the moon in that decade, recounted the origin of the company.

A son of one of the five brothers who had founded the company in 1880, Mr. Ball entitled his address "From Fruit Jars to Satellites."

Now, nearly 15 years later it still might be appropriate to say that the story of Ball could be expressed with the words: "From Fruit Jars to Satellites." However the company embraces

THE FIVE BALL BROTHERS

| GEORGE A. BALL | LUCIUS L. BALL | FRANK C. BALL | EDMUND B. BALL | WILLIAM C. BALL |
| 1862-1955 | 1850-1932 | 1857-1943 | 1855-1925 | 1852-1921 |

(Plate 7.) Taken during the 1880s.

[1]

(Plate 8.) The brothers pose again in 1913 in their Muncie office.

much more. In 1969, Ball Brothers Company, Inc. became Ball Corporation, a widely-diversified, multi-industry complex, operating worldwide.

Ball Corporation today is the world's largest and the best-known manufacturer of fruit jars. In 1974 the company produced more jars and fittings than in any year of its illustrious history. Over the 90 years since the first jars were produced in Buffalo, New York, Ball has made more jars and fittings than all other fruit jar manufacturers combined.

Today fruit jars are eagerly sought by homemakers to preserve the bounty and goodness of earth's produce and labor's rewards.

Today, also, fruit jars are eagerly sought as "collectibles" by men, women and children who see in them something quite desirable.

Ball started with the young brothers in western New York, full of hope and enterprise, short of cash and long on determination. Proud and responsible, they put their name on their business. Successive generations of consumers have liked and respected that honest boldness.

The story is told of their initial failures and then their early successes with a tin-jacketed glass jug for carrying kerosene or coal oil — then the popular source of illumination. Manufacture of their own glass jugs left them with surplus glass capacity.

In 1884, four years after the company was founded, they turned to making fruit jars. The famous Mason patent had expired five years earlier. Dozens of other little glassworks were making fruit jars. But the first of the Ball jars did not follow the pattern, set by other jar makers, of using John L. Mason's name and the word "patent" and the "Nov. 30, 1858" date on the face of the jar. The Ball brothers used the now-famous BBGMCo monogram on their first jars.

These are the so-called "Buffalo jars" and were made for only part of three years in 1884, 1885 and 1886 until a fire destroyed the little factory at 10-32 Porter Street. They had begun at 29 Hanover Street and were burned out. Next they were at 55 Main Street where the office remained until the Porter Street factory was begun.

The Buffalo jar was made in both amber and aqua and in sizes ranging from the half-gallon down to the pint and midget. Only four amber "Buffalo" jars are known to exist.

Until recently, it was believed there were only three differently embossed styles of Buffalo jars: two variations of the monogram, one with the ascenders and descenders of the "M" extending beyond the limits of the "C" as is shown in plate 8, and the other with the entire "M" contained with the "C," and a third which shows the "M" and the "G" extending above and below the "BB" and "Co", with the word PORCELAIN arched above and the word LINED on a horizontal below.

The rarest Buffalo jar shows the monogram again, similar to the one in plate 9 with the word BALL arched above the monogram and the words FRUIT JAR with all of the letters capitalized but the letters "B" and "F" in larger capitals. This jar is in the quart size and has the usual zinc band and glass lid found with other Buffalo jars. This jar, the only one of its kind known, was donated to the Ball museum by Mrs. Dorothy R. Powers, in memory of her sister, Miss Sybil Randall, its most recent owner.

The glass lids carry the inscription around the circumference of the top "Ball Brothers Glass Mfg Co Buffalo, N.Y." They come in aqua, flint and milk glass.

The Porcelain Lined jar, of course, was not porcelain lined; however, the cap, a conventional Mason threaded screw cap, did have a milk glass liner unlike the other Buffalo jars.

(*Plate 9.*) The "Buffalo" with the Ball Brothers' famous BBGMCo monogram. This jar and lid date from 1884 or 1885 and are among the first made by the brothers in their Buffalo factory on Porter Street. This monogram is one of at least three versions. This is a half-gallon.

(*Plate 10.*) These two pint "Buffalo" jars show some of the variation in these early containers. The one at left shows the beautiful whittled look of having been made in a wooden mold. At right is a midget, narrow mouth, pint with one of the monogram variations with the addition of words below and above the insignia. This jar was probably made in 1886 or 1887.

(*Plate 11.*) The same two pints as shown illustrates two more different types of closures found with Buffalo jars. At left is a milk glass lid and zinc screw band. The lid has the lettering of Ball Bros. Glass Mfg. Co. Buffalo, N. Y. The jar cap at right is zinc with a porcelain liner, again with the same lettering as the lid at left.
The "Porcelain Lined" jar, of course, was not lined with porcelain.
That referred to the cap.

It may be assumed the BBGMCo monograms were made in 1884-1885 and the Porcelain Lined and Ball Fruit Jar versions were additions to the line in 1886. There are some respected collectors, however, who now believe that perhaps the Buffalo jar may have been revived in the early Muncie days — or perhaps made in Buffalo where Ball maintained some operations into the 1890s, after the Muncie move. There is also speculation about jars having been made in Bath, New York, where Ball had operations in the 1890s, but these were metal-working operations and not glassmaking plants. No jars were ever again made by Ball in Buffalo or ever in Bath.

The "wordless" Buffalo jars carry a beautiful whittled look as though they were made in wooden molds. The other varieties look as if they were made in metal molds.

Production for 1886 was 12,500 gross (144) jars and 17,500 gross for the following year before the fire destroyed the factory.

The brothers — originally it was Frank C. and Edmund B., who were later joined in business by George A., William C., and Lucius L. (who later became a physician) — sent Frank, the company's president, to explore sites for the new factory after the fire.

Natural gas had been discovered in western Pennsylvania, Ohio and Indiana. Frank C. Ball visited many of the communities which then, as now, were hungry for industry. One which he liked was Findlay, Ohio, where the company located a metal container plant in 1973. Edmund B. Ball visited Muncie, Indiana, and then both he and Frank returned for a closer look. As F. C. was weighing offers from Findlay and Fostoria, Ohio, he received a telegram from Muncie and he returned to the little city in east central Indiana. The business leaders of the city apparently greeted him with more cordiality and seriousness of purpose than others.

The deal was struck to provide the young brothers with $7,500 — about $1.25 per citizen in those days — to defray moving expenses from Buffalo, seven acres of land on which to build, and free gas for five years. The gas well was "brought in" on September 9, 1887.

That deal may have been the most important decision ever made for the economic and cultural future of the community. Ball continued to make glass in Muncie from that start until 1962 and still manufactures home canning lids and a wide variety of sophisticated electronic equipment used in glassmaking there. The city is the location of the company's international headquarters today.

The intertwining of the names Ball and Muncie was forever solidified, so much so that it is impossible to write of Muncie without mentioning Ball or vice versa.

Construction of the new plant, located then as now in the southeast corner of the city, began in 1887, and the first glass was made March 1, 1888. The first glass made that day was oil containers and lamp chimneys, however, not fruit jars.

Natural gas brought scores of new industries to Muncie and other cities in the Gas Belt. Other glass companies sprang up like mushrooms in the Hoosier spring. Gas was so abundant that it burned day and night — turning the cloudless nights into artificial noons — and was thought to be inexhaustible.

As gas that brought industry finally was depleted, most of the boom companies folded or moved. Ball remained.

The need for glassmaking molds was apparently acute at the beginning of the Muncie operation from those early years. We have examples of many different kinds of jars and embossings being used with the addition of the Ball name to the top of the front of the jar or on the back. The flying start which the new plant achieved can be indicated by the fact that daily production reached 80 gross of jars that first year. The sand came from Millington, Illinois; the lime from Fostoria, Ohio; and the soda ash from England. Soda ash at that time came to America as ships' ballast from England and Belgium.

It is most probable that the so-called Christmas Mason was an acquired mold. The front carries the legend "MASON PATENT 30th 58" with each letter in MASONS PATENT having lines drawn vertically through them capped on each end with a dot — giving the embossing a "Christmasy" ornamentation. The back, obviously cut by another mold maker with a very businesslike hand, has the letters THE BALL in an arch over the word JAR. The front embossing is nearly smooth and ill-defined; the reverse is prominently raised and well-defined.

The use of Ball in so-called Gothic capital letters on various kinds of molds continued until mid-1892 when the first of the scripts came into being.

Much has been written and more surmised about the Ball script, perhaps one of the best-known company trademarks in the world.

Some have said that it is how William C. Ball wrote his surname. A comparison here of the signatures of the five brothers may be of some help to prove all such theories incorrect.

Frank C. Ball

Edmund B. Ball

George A. Ball

William C. Ball

Lucius L. Ball

In 1892 the block letters gave way to a script such as is seen in plate 12 written in a straight horizontal line — sometimes with and sometimes without an underscore — but never a connected underscore with the final ''L''.

Most of the jars from this era seem to be ones which found Ball adopting the use of the ''MASONS PATENT 1858'' words on the front of the jar along with the name. Sometimes the date Nov. 30th was added before 1858.

(Plate 12.) The first use of the now-famous Ball script on a jar. This script without the underscore, appeared in 1893 or 1894. By this time Ball was using Mason's patent date or at least his name on almost all its jars, perhaps because of some "mystique" by the consumers or competition.

(Plate 13.) The scripted name now had an underscore — not connected, however, and with the broad end of the score on the right instead of the later thickening on the left. Note the straight shoulders of this pint.

(Plate 14.) These two aqua quarts also show the script with the disconnected underscore. The shoulders have some slope to them. Note the variation in color and the bubbles. These jars are about 1894-1895.

(Plate 15.) More early Muncie jars, made from acquired and reworked molds. At the left the letters THE BALL are much sharper than the rest of the lettering. The jar at the right was made from a mold very similar to that one used at left but it was nearer "retirement age" at the time this jar was made. These are of the period 1888-1893.

(Plate 16.) A rather common half-gallon until the legend on the back is read in conjunction with a letter which it contained as found in the Ball Museum. The letter, by Frank C. Ball, indicates that Ball made the jar in 1890. It had been in continuous use in a Minnesota family for 35 years when it was sent to him in 1925. "I recognize the Jar as one produced by us about 35 years ago and will be very glad to list it with some of our other relics that we have on hand. The Jar certainly illustrates the durability of our glass," Mr. Ball wrote.
"I remember making my first trip to the Twin Cities a little over 35 years ago and at that time I secured orders from nearly all the wholesale grocery and queensware trade in business there. Probably this Jar was shipped on one of these orders," he continued. "The Jar reminds me of an incident which occurred on this trip. In those days silk hats were worn and, wanting to make a favorable impression, I purchased my first silk hat in Chicago. When I reached the Twin Cities there was a blizzard and the thermometer stood about forty degrees below zero. Men were wearing fur caps and fur coats. Realizing that I was badly out of style and with my ears nearly frozen, I broke for a hat store and purchased a fur cap, discarding the silk hat which I have never had the courage to wear on a business trip since. It seems a long time ago but this Jar brings it all back to me."

(Plate 17.) One of the very first jars made in Muncie after leaving Buffalo. This jar, which has the Masons Patent Nov 30th 1858 designation on the front, is shown here with BALL embossed on the reverse. This is obviously an acquired mold.

(Plate 18.) The Ball Christmas Mason jar. Jar at left shows the typical "Christmas Mason" type of lettering. The jar at right, made by Ball in Muncie, used a mold with identical "Christmasy" lettering on the obverse and the words "THE BALL JAR" cut into the back side of the mold. This jar would date sometime between 1888 and 1892 or 1893.

(Plate 19.) "The Mason" is a well-known jar. It is one of the earlier uses of script on a jar. Ball obviously acquired the mold and used it for a jar known to collectors as "Ball The Mason." This jar probably dates from 1909 and may be from an altered mold acquired with The Mason acquisition in Coffeyville, Kan., that year.

Plate 12　　　Plate 13　　　　Plate 14

Plate 15　　　　　　Plate 16

Plate 17　　Plate 18　　　　Plate 19

[9]

Plate 20

(Plate 20.) The Ball PAT APL'D FOR wire bail jar of 1895. The jar at left, owned by Norman Barnett, Flat Rock, Ind., shows the tinplated lid. The pint at right, owned by Dick Roller, Paris, Ill., shows the lid with the tinplate worn away, although the inside shows traces of tin. This jar is also known in quarts and in amber.

Plate 21

(Plate 21.) Here the "PAT APL'D FOR" jar is shown in its strangest form, at the right, as a screw top, shoulder seal jar. It was a remake of the molds made for the wire bail jars the previous season. This jar has been reported in amber. Even in aqua any of these jars are among the most desirable of all Ball-made jars.

There is evidence in the Ball Museum, in the form of a letter from Frank C. Ball, tucked inside a jar and noted on a sticker on the jar's reverse, plate 16, that he recognized the jar as one made by the company in 1890. It does not carry the name Ball at all. It is, however, recognizable by color, finish and craftsmanship, as a Ball-made jar. It was in this period that the little company was growing extremely fast and becoming a dominant force in the fruit jar business.

About 1895 Ball introduced one of the two most enigmatic jars it ever made, the one known as "The Ball PAT. APL'D. FOR."

The words "The Ball" were in horizontal script and the other words, or abbreviations, were in block letters.

This jar, always seen in aqua by me, although amber has been reported by Frank Peters (see reference list), was the forerunner of the Sure Seal-Ideal-Eclipse series. It had a wire bail, fastening fully around the neck, and took a metal lid with the legend, BALL JAR PAT APL'D FOR, embossed around the outer circumference in block letters. The amber version is owned by Roy Brown of Illinois, Chairman of the Federation of Historical Bottle Clubs.

The patent, which the jar indicates was applied for, has never been found in issued or application form. And collectors are at a loss as to what the patent claim may have been. However, it may have been a potential infringement on Henry Putnam's Lightning patent of 1882, despite the metal lid.

Dick Roller has suggested it was not Putnam's Lightning patent which may have been in conflict but potentially two others. He notes the two Hero patents of February 17, 1894, and January 29, 1895, were for closures involving small raised bumps or ridges on each side of the top to hold the bail more securely. The Ball PAT APL'D FOR lid has two parallel ridges on each side of the lid to hold the bail in place. It is highly probable that Ball was unaware of the patent applications for the Hero lids at the time the company invented the lid and started to make the jar.

Rather than scrap the mold entirely, it was remade, probably the next year, but the entire top of the mold was changed, making it into a shoulder-sealing Mason closure, with identical lettering.

Russ Willis, after this manuscript was completed, reported two additional jars made from reworked The Ball PAT. APL'D. FOR jar molds — The Ball MASONS PATENT 1858 (shoulder seal) and The Ball MASONS PATENT 1858 (obverse) and IMPROVED (reverse). "That is really getting their money out of a mold . . . evidently four different jars were made out of the original mold," he wrote.

(*Plate 22.*) An advertisement from an 1890 issue of "Pottery and Glass Works Reporter."

(*Plate 23.*) An advertisement from November 1892 issue of "Pottery and Glass Works Reporter."

F.C BALL, President.   E. B. BALL, Vice Prest.   G. A. BALL, Secy & Treas

ALL CONTRACTS AND AGREEMENTS CONTINGENT UPON STRIKES, ACCIDENTS OR OTHER CAUSES BEYOND OUR CONTROL

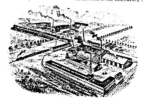

Ball Brothers Glass Mfg Co.

Fruit Jars

Muncie, Ind Feb-13/99

Plate 24

The horizontal script seems to have been used through 1896 and then faded away to be completely replaced by the now world-famous upward script, sometimes without an underscore but most often used with an underscore.

By 1897, Ball produced more than 65 percent of all the fruit jars in the United States — and was able to sell them to consumers at a price of 5 cents each. (A vastly improved jar is sold today for about 20 cents each despite 78 years' inflation.) Some were being exported that year to Africa, Norway and Australia. The company, in 1894, had begun to pack its ware in self-manufactured wooden boxes, a dozen to the box, separated by self-manufactured strawboard liners to prevent breakage.

A Muncie newspaper, in 1897, reported on a disastrous fire at the plant's warehouse which left what the paper described as "a mountainous mass of glass" two blocks long and 50 feet high. A lot of fruit jars had been reduced to waste. Hundreds of men from Muncie's "Industry" section helped fight the fire with Frank and George Ball, who sustained severe burns as they battled to save their business from another disaster similar to the one in Buffalo.

In 1907 the script Ball with a loop at the end of the second "L" was registered as a trademark of Ball Brothers Glass Manufacturing Co. on March 26 upon application of F. C. Ball, who as president, had on December 27, 1906, verified that it had "been used continuously in our business since 1894."

| Plate 25 | Plate 26 | Plate 27 |

(Plate 25.) About 1895, while the script was still horizontal,
jars were made with it beginning to slope upward to the right and with an
underscore, most often seen in earlier jars with a loop.
Here are two similar but different jars with the three-L loop showing.
These are pre-1900.

(Plate 26.) This is the so-called "Balls" or "Balle" Mason
because of the short and crude loop after the final L drops away to an underscore.
Perhaps the moldmaker's hand slipped.

This is how it looked on the trademark granted in 1907.

Ball

That mark later led to one of the most curious situations in
fruit jar history — the belief by many that Ball did not know
how to spell its own name and used three "Ls" instead of the
correct two.

Mold makers, as can be seen in the jars reproduced in this
section as well as on the filled jar on the cover, often took artistic license with the script. Sometimes the loop of the underscore was nearly upright and at times it was nearly horizontal.
One of the more interesting variations is a jar, from the author's
collection, plate 26, which has the name appearing to be spelled

Plate 28

Plate 29

Plate 30

(Plate 27.) The Whitney Mason, made by Ball for the New Jersey company, about the turn of the century. No claim is made here that Ball made all of Whitney's jars, although this one was made in Muncie.

(Plate 28.) The unimproved "Improved" Ball three-L, at left.
This jar is a standard Mason shoulder sealing Mason jar and is not related to either Mason's improved jar or to the Ball Improved of a later vintage. There seems to be a close relationship between these two jars pictured here.

(Plate 29.) Not normally regarded as a prized jar, this flint Ball three-L Mason is identical in all respects to the one on its side at the right, except for the base. It is blank. The one at the right, made in aqua, was one of the first special order jars Ball made. This one was for Hahne & Co., Newark, N.J., and is a very important Ball jar.

(Plate 30.) Aqua and green pints and quarts were made with only the name shown. These are the "purest" forms of the three-L jars — without any other words on the jar.

(Plate 31.) An advertisement from the August, 1904 issue of "Woman's Home Companion."

"BALL MASON" FRUIT JARS.

There is a difference in the Mason Fruit Jars made by various manufacturers. "BALL MASON" Fruit Jars are the best because they are made of the best material, by skilled workmen. The Jars are carefully selected, provided with perfect Caps and good Rubbers. They are thoroughly reliable and will keep fruit for years.

Why take chances of your fruit spoiling by using inferior or untried brands? The "BALL MASON" has been used over 20 years, is known to be reliable, and can be obtained at a reasonable price. More of them are used than all other brands combined. This fact is evidence of their superiority.

Demand "BALL MASON" Jars.

BALL BROS. GLASS MFG. CO., - MUNCIE, IND.
Largest Fruit Jar Mfrs. in the World.

Balls or Balle with an underscore. The "s" or "e" is nothing more than a mold maker's variation.

Despite this, however, so-called 3-L jars fetch prices probably beyond their comparative value to other jars in the Ball series.

In 1898 the F. C. Ball machine was perfected, giving Ball Brothers a technological advantage over most other jar manufacturers. The blow pipe method of producing jars yielded 10 gross in 10 hours using five workmen. With the F. C. Ball machine, three men could make 50 gross in the same time — a productivity increase of 734 percent!

The company's leaders had long been interested in processes to make better products and in 1894 or 1895 Ball had purchased some of the early and primitive semi-automatic glass-blowing machines invented by Charles E. Blue of Wheeling, West Virginia.

The F. C. Ball machine far surpassed the Blue machine in technical sophistication, although both were hand indexed or rotated by hand to push the blank mold into position for the next gob of molten glass. In the next two years, work continued to improve the F. C. Ball machine. Beginning in 1900 and until 1906 when new patents were issued, the work was carried on by F. C. Ball and A. L. Bingham, a nephew of the brothers' mother, Maria Bingham Ball. The Ball-Bingham machine was a revolution in the glass industry. It did everything except bring glass to the machine and carry the finished bottle away. It was completely automatic and further increased productivity by massive proportions.

During this time, Ball advertised in the August 1904 issue of the "Woman's Home Companion" that it was the "Largest Fruit Jar Mfrs in the World." See plate 31. (Also note in this ad the use of the word "perfect" which may have been the first time it appeared in Ball sales material but which was to become one of the most important parts of Ball promotion and salesmanship.)

Julian Toulouse and Dick Roller, one in print and the other in conversation, have strongly implied that they believe Ball did not abandon the F. C. Ball machine overnight and turn to the Ball-Bingham machine suddenly one morning. It was a gradual phasing out of the old and a phasing in of the new. A hallmark of the Ball operation has always been never to waste anything of value — for after all they were in the business of helping people save, preserve and conserve (if readers will allow me to use the double meanings of the latter two words).

Ball in 1903 acquired an option to obtain exclusive license to make fruit jars by the Owens machine, invented by Michael

(Plate 32.) The Ball-Bingham machine in operation in Ball's glass plant about 1903.

J. Owens. This marvel of glassmaking reportedly had 10,000 parts and weighed 100,000 pounds. The company allowed the option to expire because it believed its·machines were comparable in quality and cost.

Owens then licensed Louis Hollweg of Greenfield, Indiana, to use the machine and he turned it over to his company, the Greenfield Fruit Jar and Bottle Company.

In 1909 Ball acquired the Greenfield company and with its purchase came an exclusive license to make fruit jars on the Owens machines which concluded the beginning phase of Ball jar history.

The foundation had been laid; the company was the dominant force in the fruit jar business — as it would remain for the next six decades.

The next phase was that of merger and acquisition, some of which began shortly after the turn of the century, and some of which would continue into 1936 with companies and 1933 with acquisition of distinctive features.

Paralleling the merger and acquisition era were two other phases. These are best divided, for jar collectors' purposes, into two sections — the screw top jars and the wire bail jars. These two types ran parallel until 1962.

Plate 33

II

Becoming a Household Word

As early as 1906 Ball was not only the dominant force in fruit jars in America but the company had become a major exporter of jars and fittings to Europe, South Africa and Australia. This exporting continued for many years, to a greater or lesser degree, until the beginning of World War II.

Late in 1974, Edmund F. Ball, his sister, Mrs. John W. Fisher, and Mrs. Ball and Mr. Fisher, were traveling in Australia. While there they visited a restored pioneer village in Jindera, New South Wales. In the museum there, they discovered a Ball Mason, one Mr. Ball estimated was made in Muncie about 1910.

When Edmund F. Ball joined the family-owned company in 1928, one of his wintertime jobs was to pack wooden boxes with jars and fill the boxes with straw for shipment to South Africa and Australia where the canning season is opposite that in the northern hemisphere.

In the summer of 1974, Ball Corporation was asked to donate fruit jars of the 1906-1912 era to the Woodrow Wilson House in Washington, D. C. With that presentation, Ball President John W. Fisher said in a letter to the president of the National Trust for Historic Preservation,

(*Plate 34.*) Ball's first president and its current president are shown in this 1942 photograph. At left is John W. Fisher, now president of the company. He was accompanying Frank C. Ball on a tour of the Muncie operations when this was made. Mr. Ball was president from the 1880 founding until his death in 1943 — 63 years. Barely visible in the background, to Mr. Fisher's left, is Mr. Ball's youngest brother, George A. Ball, who became president in 1943 and served until his death in 1955.

"Ball's own research and that sponsored by Ball at university centers also pioneered food preservation technology which is still used today. This early work had great impact on this nation's ability to preserve its perishable harvests so that its people could enjoy an ever-increasing standard of living.

"The homemaker's favorable experience with home canned foods led to her acceptance of commercially preserved foods. Many well-known food products in grocery markets today started from a favorite recipe of a good cook using Ball jars."

Later in this book we will examine some of the private "label" jars Ball made for its customers which led the company into the manufacture of commercial glass containers.

The forerunner to today's *Blue Book* was first compiled and written in 1905. Miss Elisabeth Ball, daughter of George A. Ball and his wife, Frances Woodworth Ball, was "present at the creation," as she put it in a recent conversation.

"Father wrote all of the directions. Mother gathered all of the recipes from her own files, from her family and from friends so she knew all of them had been tried or used and were satisfactory," Miss Ball related.

"I was about eight years of age and was quite proud and thrilled that Father and Mother were doing something very good.

"We did quite a little doing here in our kitchen to try out the recipes and the methods to know they were all right.

"It was largely a family affair. Father wanted to be absolutely sure that everything in the book was correct. I so wish I had a copy of it today.

"Later there were many requests for recipes not included in the book so Father finally turned it over to a professional cook. He insisted on the testing which has continued to this day," Miss Ball recalled.

Miss Ball's wish for a first edition of the predecessor volume to the earliest-known book is one voiced by many collectors.

The earliest-known version, called *The Correct Method for Preserving Fruit*, was published in 1909 and contains recipes for vegetables as well as fruit. Interestingly, the cover was green, not blue. Later editions were called *The Correct Methods . . .*, adding a plural to the word method.

The *Blue Books* were revised yearly, or more often, in the years up to America's plunge into World War I in 1917.

America sought to stay out of the "European" war, with Wilson winning reelection in 1916 on a slogan of "He Kept Us Out of War". It was only a few months, however, before we plunged in — to end the madness, once and for all we thought.

America, in 1906 under Theodore Roosevelt, through 1920 under Wilson and Mrs. Wilson, the first surrogate President, was a blossoming nation. Our economic and industrial revolution was raising our standard of living to the highest in the world. Our population was growing by leaps and bounds. We brought into the Union the last three remaining continental territories, Oklahoma in 1907 and Arizona and New Mexico in 1912.

It was Ball who was there to help feed a hungry nation and "to tell its homemakers how."

Ball made fine products for home food preservation; Ball knew how to sell the products; Ball provided the research to make the products work. And it goes without saying that a company with such a famous name, which put its name on every one of its products, stood behind its wares.

In the 70 years of *Blue Books* they have been given or sold to millions of homemakers and if my estimates are correct it is

(*Plate 35.*) This drawing of the Ball Brothers Glass Manufacturing Company facilities in Muncie was made sometime prior to 1903 and looks to the south and southwest.

BALL BROTHERS GLASS MFG. CO.

FACTORIES
MUNCIE , IND.
TERRE HAUTE,IND.

FRUIT JARS
AND
BOTTLES

GREENFIELD,IND.
COFFEYVILLE, KAS.
LA HARPE KAS.

·MUNCIE·IND·

Plate 36

probably one of the most-widely printed English works in the world.

Much has been made among a few collectors about Ball's acquisition of other glass companies. However, a brief look at the number of automobile brands extant in the early days of this century, and the subsequently diminished number existing at the time of World War II, will show a similar pattern.

Many glass companies sprang up throughout the Midwestern Gas Belt and died when the gas ran out. Ball acquired a few of those which had facilities, technologies or markets which met its own criteria for excellence.

One of the early Gas Boom bust casualties was the Marion Fruit Jar and Bottle Company, Marion, Indiana, which also had factories in Fairmount, Indiana; Converse, Indiana; and Coffeyville, Kansas. Ball purchased Marion in 1904 and operated it and the other Hoosier plants until about 1910. Coffeyville remained important for a longer time, until perhaps 1913, when it and the Mason Fruit Jar & Bottle Co., Coffeyville, bought in 1909, and perhaps another company, the Premium Glass Company of Coffeyville, purchased by Ball in 1912, (if it actually was acquired) became the foundation for a new plant in Wichita Falls, Texas. Another plant, the Texas Bottle Co., there had been purchased in 1913 and may have been part of the Wichita Falls operation.

The Coffeyville location was abandoned because of a failure in the natural gas supply. Years later, as drilling equipment im-

(*Plate 37.*) The Port jar remade into a Ball jar with the alteration of the mold. The backward letters are on the front of the jar and read: Mason's Patent 1858. Note the Ball jar is in a deeper aqua than the Port which was made in Belleville, Ill., sometime between 1902 and 1904. How long Ball used this mold is not known. This Ball script is not considered a legitimate Ball script in the evolution of the company's trademark.

Plate 37

(*Plate 38.*) The Root script was reworked in its molds when Ball purchased the company in 1909. It is easy to see the exactness of the upstroke of the "R" and "B" and in the top loop of each of these letters. Jars exist which show the crossbar of the "t" under the second "l" in Ball.

Plate 38

(*Plates 39-40.*) The earliest known Perfect Masons are these with Gothic sans-serif lettering — a departure from the scripted name as it was appearing in the 1909-1910 period. These Ball jars were remakes of Boyd mold which were acquired with the purchase of the Greenfield Fruit Jar and Bottle Co., which has some type of arrangement with Illinois Glass Works, the maker of the Boyd. The italic Boyd and Ball jars here are pints and the Roman versions are quarts although they come in both sizes in both types of lettering. The italics are serif letters.

Plate 39

(*Plate 41.*) Ball's wax-sealers, probably not in the line until 1895 or 1896 — which was late for any fruit jar company to get into this semi-primitive form of sealing — was called the Standard. It is always seen with the three-L script name. The shoulders of the Ball wax sealer are more sloping than Greenfield's.

(*Plate 42.*) Greenfield's wax-sealer, the Standard, and its Mason, both carried the design device of a shepherd's crook on its side.

Plate 40

Plate 41   Plate 42

proved, more gas at the same site was found at a deeper level.

Another acquisition in 1904 was Port Glass Company, Belleville, Illinois, which had begun there in 1902 and which went out of business as a Ball operation in 1910. A comparison of the jars in plate 37 will show how Ball reworked the old Port molds into Ball molds to produce a jar with an unusual variant of the Ball script. Toulouse, in *Bottle Makers*, intimates that John W. Port may have been a Ball agent when he established his company there in 1902 with $10,000. Port, however, had operated a competing glasshouse in Muncie in 1891 onward.

In 1904 Swayzee Glass Co., Swayzee, Indiana, also near Muncie, was purchased and operated for one year.

The Upland Glass Co., Upland, Indiana, a successor to the Safe Glass Company of Upland and before that in Redkey, Indiana, was purchased in 1904 and immediately closed. Both Upland and Redkey were in the Gas Belt with Muncie, Marion, Fairmount, Converse and Swayzee.

Also acquired in 1904 was the Loogootee Fruit Jar Company in Loogootee, Indiana, which made the LGCo wax sealer jars and which was operated until 1906. Ball President John W. Fisher tells of a sheet metal building at Loogootee which was moved on to Coffeyville, then to Wichita Falls when the Ball plant was built there and afterwards moved to Okmulgee when the Texas plant closed. It is still in service at Okmulgee. Waste Not, Want Not!

Purchased in 1909 and operated for four years were the fruit jar facilities and business of the Root Glass Company, Terre Haute, Indiana. Plate 38 shows reworks of the Root mold into a Ball mold for still another unusual variation of the Ball script. This was another example of the laudable principle of "Waste Not, Want Not." Julian Toulouse mistakenly states in his book *Fruit Jars* that the Root plant was closed by Ball in 1909.

An interesting sidelight to the Root operation was that its beverage bottle operation, which Ball did not acquire, designed the first trademarked bottle used by Coca-Cola.

The most significant acquisition of this era came on November 20, 1909, when Ball purchased the Greenfield Fruit Jar and Bottle Company, Greenfield, Indiana, which had made the jars shown in plate 42; Greenfield's symbol was the shepherd's crook lying on its side with the hook on the left. Greenfield made a wax sealer and a screw-top Mason. Ball, in 1912, dropped its wax sealer, the Ball Standard, plate 41, from its line as well as the Greenfield "Standard" and the "Pint Standard" wax sealer.

(Plate 43.) An early example of a Ball Mason, made about 1910, in a light apple green. This color in Ball jars is highly collectible especially when sets of pints and half-gallons can be added to quarts such as this one.

(Plate 44.) A very late example of a 3-L jar, made with interrupted screw threads. The tinplate cap is also unusual for Ball. It appears to have been a test jar shortly after Ball began manufacturing with the Owens machine.

Plate 43   Plate 44

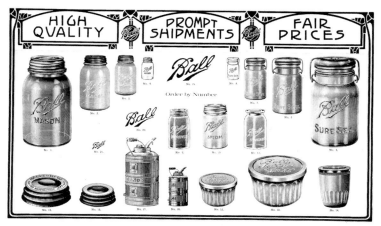

(*Plate 45.*) Ball's 1912 sales brochure offered Masons in four sizes,
half-pint to half-gallon, the Sure Seal in the same sizes, and three other jars —
the Improved (note the third L), the Special, and the wax-sealer Standard
(again with a third L). There were two squat jelly glasses and one tall,
a gallon and a half-gallon Dandy oil jug, and two sizes of zinc caps.
The reverse of this brochure indicates the company made fruit jars and bottles
and had factories in Muncie, Terre Haute and Greenfield, Ind., Coffeyville,
"Kas.", and La Harpe, "Kas." La Harpe was the site of the zinc mill.

A wax sealer is a jar with a channelled groove mouth or top.
A cork or a concave glass, ceramic, or tinplate "lid" was placed
over the opening after filling. Hot wax was poured around the
channel or groove. The wax was not beeswax or paraffin but
more like sealing wax of the times. There is some evidence that
Ball may have marketed a wax sealing ring to replace rubber
rings for sealing even the Mason jars in 1904.

The Boyd Perfect Masons were doubtless made in Greenfield,
Indiana, prior to 1909, not in Alton, Illinois, where — according to most research — they were believed made by the Illinois
Glass Co. (a predecessor of Owens-Illinois of today). See plates
39-40 for the Boyd molds which were obviously altered for
use by Ball after the acquisition that year. There are at least
five different ones.

It is unlikely that these would have originally been Ball
molds and altered for Boyd. When Illinois Glass dropped this

line, which is a Mason shoulder seal, it went to the Boyd with the Mason beaded lip seal. These Boyd, then Ball, jars were Perfect Masons, a bit of nomenclature peculiar to Ball.

Four other acquisitions, three of plants and one of an idea, round out the era of expansion.

First was the purchase of Schram Glass Manufacturing Co., St. Louis, in 1925 which was operated for several more years producing Schram jars before it was closed.

The Drey (pronounced "Dry" and named after Alexander Schram's partner, Leo Drey) Perfect Mason and the Drey Square Mason were both made by Ball for a while after the purchase of Schram, the manufacturer of the Drey brand. The Drey Perfect Masons are extremely similar to the Ball Perfect Masons and are excellent examples of Ball craftsmanship.

The Square Mason line was picked up by Ball and made for at least a few years in large quantities, judging by the number of them still available. The molds, at least originally, were re-works of the Drey molds and in all of the sizes, except the pint, they show the embossing of a carpenter's square on the front of the jar. The pint was too small to get the carpenter's square on its face.

Schram had plants in Hillsboro, Illinois, operated until 1961 when it was sold by Ball; Huntington, West Virginia, closed before World War II; and Sapulpa, Oklahoma, operated until 1931. The land was sold in 1940. The Sapulpa facilities were merged in 1931 with other facilities at Okmulgee, Oklahoma.

Next came the purchase in 1929 of Pine Glass Co., Okmulgee, Oklahoma, the only acquired location where Ball still operates a glass plant. That year Pine was making a jar called the Pine Deluxe Jar, one of three it made during its three-year history. The letters on the jar were highly embossed, having an almost prismatic effect.

Again, Ball reworked this mold and made for one year, the Ball Deluxe Jar. See plate 47. Examining the Ball jar closely it is easy to see the "filled in" upper horizontals of the "E" on the final "L". You can also see that the mold maker did not

Plate 46

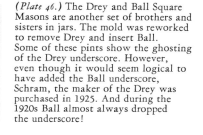

(*Plate 46.*) The Drey and Ball Square Masons are another set of brothers and sisters in jars. The mold was reworked to remove Drey and insert Ball. Some of these pints show the ghosting of the Drey underscore. However, even though it would seem logical to have added the Ball underscore, Schram, the maker of the Drey was purchased in 1925. And during the 1920s Ball almost always dropped the underscore!

Plate 47

(*Plate 47.*) Certainly not the most valuable, but perhaps one of the most beautiful of all Ball jars is the BALL DELUXE JAR, shown here with its sister jar, the PINE DELUXE. Unfortunately these show a round jar contrasted with a square jar. However, the mold reworking was similar. The "P" had a crude second loop added. The upper parts of the "E" were not quite eradicated and the new plate behind the "AL" of Ball does not entirely hide the "IN" of Pine.

(*Plate 48.*) The grip bars or grippers came with the license from Brockway in 1933. They were probably put on the jars in 1934 because they are photographed in the Blue Book early in 1935. Here we see a 1920s Perfect Mason without them, then the Brockway Sur-Grip Mason with the convenient device, then the Ball Perfect Mason with them with Ball shown with and without the underscore for the name. A Museum jar with a Vacu-Seal lid, marked 1934 for the date of the first two-piece metal lid, is an underscored Ball with the grip marks on the jar, identical to the jar at the right.

[29]

(Plate 49.) The "Ball Mason's Patent," with the name not underscored was made by Ball from molds acquired in the Schram purchase. The jar on the left, from the Ball Museum, was made in Sapulpa, Okla., on May 19, 1927. This is still more evidence to support the theory that the underscore was dropped all during the '20s.

make the bottom loop of the "B" as precisely as the top loop had been made when it was a "P". More careful examination will show a faint "I" and "N" behind the "A" and first "L". The jar was made in both the round and square shapes.

The acquisition of the design feature, perhaps one of the most important from a convenience standpoint for the home canner, was the purchase of the patent from Brockway Glass Co. in 1933 of the Sure-Grip or vertical gripper marks for the jars. See plate 48. Ball phased them in on all of the Mason finish jars but did not use them on the wire bail jars. A certain way of narrowing the dating of the aqua Ball Perfect Masons is that all jars without grippers are pre-1933 and those with grippers are no earlier than 1933 and no later than 1937 when the aqua or Ball blue color was discontinued. The gripper-marked jars show up early in 1935 in the *Blue Book*.

Ball purchased Three Rivers Glass Company, Three Rivers, Texas, in 1937, rebuilt it and operated it briefly until demand fell to a point where it had to be closed. It was never reopened by Ball before its sale.

Nearly four decades of acquisitions came to a close shortly before the outbreak of World War II. The company had made millions and millions of fruit jars, in more than a dozen cities and towns across America, most of them in Muncie, shipped first in wooden boxes and then paperboard cartons (see plates 118-122). Ball in the 1890s had become the first company to ship a dozen of anything to the grocery trade, creating a marketing revolution.

In 1902 and beyond, a little-known railroad's rolling stock became known, leaving Muncie loaded with jars. The Muncie and Western Railroad, familiarly known as the Ball Line, sent its yellow boxcars (see plate 51) into every state. The M&WRR,

(Plate 50.)
This model of one of
the box cars is owned by
Alexander M. Bracken,
president of the
Muncie & Western, and former
general counsel of Ball.
Mr. Bracken, now Ball's board
chairman as well as president of
the Ball State University board
of trustees, has long been one of
the key figures in Ball's growth.
The Ball jar here,
in a Kelly green, is typical
of the millions of jars which
went to every part of the
nation in these rail cars.

(Plate 51.) Countless millions of jars rolled out of Muncie over the years from 1902 until 1962 in the famous yellow box cars of the Muncie & Western Railroad, known as the Ball Line. This photograph of one of the last of the cars is owned by Elmer Cox, superintendent of the Muncie & Western.

or MWR as it is known by railroads and rail buffs, still exists, linking the Muncie operations together, nine blocks north to south and seven blocks east to west — the world's shortest railroad. In 1933, there were many days when Ball shipped more than 100 full boxcars of its wares from Muncie as well as many truck loads.

During this period Ball had seen a nation through war, normalcy, prosperity and then a crushing depression. There are countless thousands of Americans today who can tell stories of how survival literally was tied to the number of Ball jars their mothers or grandmothers could fill with the fruit, vegetables and meat they could raise or hunt in summer and fall.

In 1973, the elderly widow of a Methodist minister sent the company a quart of canned rabbit meat she had put up when she was a young woman and her husband was serving a Missouri circuit in the 1920s.

Ball jars of that era have emerged from the survival category. And it is no wonder that they are held in such esteem and with such affection as they are today. Perhaps nostalgia and the subconscious practice of the philosophy of existentialism have something to do with it.

Today's homemaker, faced with escalating food prices, can watch her money as well as satisfy that deep sense of creativity by turning to home canning. She will use modern jars — marked by Ball and only Ball for the first time in 1974 — with metric measurements on the right side of wide mouth and regular quarts and regular pints to correspond to the cups and ounces markings on the left. But somewhere in that kitchen she will proudly display a jar or jars used by her mother or grandmother, perhaps as canisters as Mrs. Beth Bowen, wife of Indiana's governor has, or as terraria to brighten a dark corner.

If she really becomes avid about it, that collection will grow and will take an honored place in the family room or living room over a fireplace mantel, in a bookcase or in a special window.

Amazingly, however, most jar collectors are not women.

III

A Clear Choice

With the acquisition of the Owens license, Ball began its greatest period of growth as a fruit jar company and began producing its greatest number of distinctly different jars.

However, they may be most easily divided into two groups — those with the screw or Mason seal, and those with a wire bail, glass top, rubber gasket fastening arrangement.

This gave the homemaker a clear choice. She could use what she wanted from the widest line of safe home canning jars ever offered in the world.

Because these two types of jars utilized such distinctly different closures they should be treated separately.

It is interesting at this point to correct some popular misconceptions by stating some facts:

1. John L. Mason, born 1832 and who died in 1902, never worked for Ball; nor did Ball acquire his company or his patent.

2. All Ball jars are not Mason jars; all Mason jars are not Ball jars.

3. Ball jars were made in blue, but they were also made in other colors — flint (clear), amber, green, aqua and pink. (A single run of pink occurred by accident at Ball's Asheville, N. C., plant in the early 1970s.) The aqua, green, blue and Ball blue colors were variations occurring naturally according to origin of ingredients and were not "controlled" colors, according to Edmund F. Ball.

4. Ball did not make amethyst or smoky gray jars. Jars which are that color were made in flint and the sun's rays, acting on trace minerals in the glass, turned the jars these unusual colors. Other flint jars have been found in "sunstruck" pink and honey amber.

5. Ball made no jars in 1858. It did not make the Ideal jar or the Sure Seal or the Sanitary Sure Seal on July 14, 1908. That is the date of an obscure and confused patent, which may or may not have had something to do with those jars.

6. "Dated" fruit jars are not really dated, except for a very few commemorative issues. The Ball Ideal Bicentennial jar, which was made beginning December 2, 1974, carries the number "75" on its base. This indicates that it was made about 1975. This and maybe one or two other "dated"

Plate 52   Plate 53

(Plate 52.) The color jars add distinction to any collection.
These are a few of the very unusual colors available in Ball-made glass jars.
Top: Two shades of amber, left and right, very dark made at Hillsboro, Ill., between 1956 and 1961, and center, a medium amber, made in the 1930s.
The line down the face of the jar is a defect.

(Plate 53.) The three-L Mason on the left is aqua streaked with amber, probably made during a color change in a glass tank. Jar at right is a light lavender colored that way by exposure of the original flint glass to the sun. Note the artistic loop.

commemorative jars are actually of the time of the dates they carry.

Jar collecting can always be fun unless the collector is stung by someone who is less than candid and truthful.

(*Plate 54.*) Five very unusual colors, from left, a green <u>Balll</u> Standard, a purple Standard of later vintage, a light lavender Sure Seal, a rose pink Sure Seal, and a very dark smoky brown Ideal. The wire contraption above the jars is a Ball-made jar lifter from about 1920.

(*Plate 55.*) A matched set of Perfect Masons in an unusual olive green, used as kitchen canisters by Mrs. Norman Barnett, Flat Rock, Ind.

IV

A While to Become Ideal

Ball's entry into the wire bail jar market, to complement its dominance of the screw top jar market, had occurred about 1895 with the jar known as The Ball PAT. APL'D. FOR. It had a full twisted wire bail and required a sheet metal cap. An example, belonging to Norman Barnett of Flat Rock, Indiana, shows the metal top to have been plated with a material resembling tin.

The company's patent files fail to reveal what the patent was or if it really was applied for. In any event, the patent was never issued, if the various fruit jar patent researchers are correct.

In 1908, however, a patent was issued to Anthony F. McDonnell of Dunmore, Pennsylvania, on July 14. The patent was for full, round dimples on the side of a glass container (a bottle, not a jar, is shown in the McDonnell application) into which the locking lever of the bail was fastened.

That date, July 14, 1908, is the second date most-commonly known in fruit jar history — the other being Mason's Nov. 30, 1858.

The ubiquitous date is also the bane of advanced collectors who try to educate the novice that the date does not mean the jar was made that day, which many believe!

(*Plate 56.*) The Ball Sure Seals with full wire twisted-tie bail.

(*Plates 57-58.*)
The Ball Sanitary Sure Seals.
Two jars in left photograph show two different types of neck finish with snap-in bails and neck lugs, similar to those described in McDonnell patent of July 14, 1908. Base of jar on right shows the crude lettering of PAT'D JULY 14, 08. This is the only known form of the patent date on the Sanitary Sure Seals.

Plate 56

Plate 57

Plate 58

The odd thing about the patent date, which Ball used on many of its jars, is that it was not used on the earliest of these jars in 1908 or 1909. And, too, it was used on jars which had the full twisted wire tie bail (without the circular dimples) and on jars with hemispherical lugs.

It appeared on the front of quarts and half-gallons and on the front and back of pints. It also appeared on the base of some jars.

The first of the glass lid, wire bail Ball jars of the 20th century was the Sure Seal series. The earliest known *Blue Books* show the Sure Seal as the Standard line-items with the screw top Mason jars until 1915.

(Plate 59.) A wide range of square Ball Ideal jars.
From the left, the Southern Methodist Orphans Home half-gallon (embossing on reverse), then a pair of square Ideal quarts with full wire bails, the second of which has the patent date on the obverse, then two pints with the bail attached by insertion into the half-hemisphere lugs as with the Southern Methodist jar. The patent date on the third jar is one of the mysteries because the bail is not attached as the patent would indicate it should be.

But somewhere between 1908 and 1915, and perhaps paralleling the Sure Seal the entire time, the Sanitary Sure Seal was produced — identical in every respect to its sister-jar except for the italicized word SANITARY.

Plates 57-58 show the patented feature on two different types of neck on Sanitary Sure Seals but these jars do not carry the patent date. However, another very similar jar — in the Sanitary Sure Seal series — carries the date on the bottom in crude lettering, plate 58.

Mrs. Alice Creswick in her *Red Book of Fruit Jars No. 2* lists a Sure Seal in flint, although Frank Peters in his *Fruit Jar Manual* does not. And although the author has never seen a Sure Seal in flint, nor does the Ball Museum contain one, Ball did have flint capacity as early as 1890 in its No. 2 plant in Muncie. Russ Willis indicates flint Sure Seals can be found on the West Coast.

It is possible that the Sanitary Sure Seal was a specially-made jar for a jobber or retail outlet. No evidence of this has been

(*Plate 60.*) Two Ideal pints, one without the patent date, left, and the other with it on the reverse, right.

(*Plate 61.*) The Southern Methodist jar, made only in half-gallons.

Plate 60

Plate 61

found, although speculation can be grounded in the fact that *Blue Books* (not called that name until 1915 with edition G, published in July that year) and sales literature of the era mention only the Sure Seal.

The *Blue Book* went through edition H also in 1915, but with edition J in 1916, the Sure Seal was gone. A note with the Ball Museum collection of *Blue Books* indicates that George A. Ball had sorted and numbered them and concluded there was no edition I, probably skipped because of the confusion with the numeral 1.

In place of the Sure Seal, inside the front cover illustrated next to the Ball Perfect Mason, is the Ball Ideal. However, in edition D in 1913 the name Ideal had been used with Ball's Ideal Family Jelly Glasses — and that's probably where the name originated.

The wire bail jar had taken 20 years to become Ideal. Over the next 47 years the Ideal became one of the half-dozen, best-known glass containers in history and one of the most prized.

Since its discontinuance 12 or 13 years ago in 1962, the Ideal has remained in service with the sale of rubber rings for use in canning remaining active, especially in the northeastern United States where its popularity was always the greatest.

(Plate 62.) A wide range of round Ball Ideals,
showing different forms of the Ball script in sizes from quart to pint to
one-third pint, second from right, to half-pint, right. The half-pint is a
sun-struck honey amber flint. Lack of underscore would indicate it
was made in the 1920s, however, it has a bail arrangement of much
earlier form.

It was made in aqua, Ball blue and flint and in a variety of
sizes, half-gallon, quart, pint, half-pint, and one-third pint. It
was made in round and "square" and with and without the
patent dates. It had all three types of wire bails — the half-
round or hemispherical, the full-circular lug and the full twisted
wire. All took the same size lid, however.

One of the more unusual ones was a special order half-gallon
for the Southern Methodist Orphans Home. The reverse of the
jar carries the embossing, see plate 61, Property of Southern
Methodist Orphans Home Waco, Texas. Estimates of the date
of its manufacture range from 1922 to 1932.

Another wire bail Ball jar — this one without the traditional
script (which was sometimes underscored and sometimes not)
is the Ball Deluxe Jar. This is a remake of the mold acquired
with the Pine Glass Company in Okmulgee, Oklahoma, in 1929.
It is considered one of the most glamorous of all Ball jars because of its unique, prismatic embossed letters.

Between 1926 and 1930 or, more properly, between edition N
and edition O of the *Blue Book*, another jar had come along —
the Eclipse.

The Eclipse, commonly believed to be merely a wide-mouth
Ideal, certainly did not start that way. In plate 66 it is shown

with a regular mouth, a full-wire bail, and is in a faint blue glass and carries a patent date of 7-14-08 on the base. It also does not have the traditional slash under the Ball name, rather common from illustrations in *Blue Books* of the 1920s. This jar was also made in flint and Ball blue.

By 1930, however, the Eclipse Wide Mouth in half-gallons, quarts and pints had arrived. It, too, was to stay in the Ball line until 1962.

All I have seen are round and in flint, although they may have come in colors. They do have the hemispherical dimple for the bail. The July 14, 1908, date does appear on the reverse of the pint in some examples. Plate 65 shows this in the jar at the right. Note also the different bottom configurations of the two quarts in the middle of the photograph.

It has come as a shock to some collectors to find a very unusual wide-mouth glass lid — for an Eclipse jar. This lid is marked with the Ball script, underscored, and has the date 1915 on its top. The piece of glass is cobalt blue!

About 200 of these were made in 1969 or 1970 by members of the glass research lab at the Muncie technical division as favors given at the annual shareholders meeting that year. A few of these have subsequently reached the collecting market and have been the cause of intense and immense consternation. They had immediately set out in search of a never-made cobalt Ball Eclipse jar.

(Plates 63-64.) Ball blue Ideals, without underscore for the script, probably made in the 1920s. The jar at right shows the patent date on the front. The square jar, now one of the most collectible of the Ideals, is without the patent date, although both of these jars have the half-lug bail attachment device.

Plate 63   Plate 64

The story of the Ideal jar is far from over, however. Ball President John W. Fisher has long been a fan of the Ideal jar and has frequently suggested its revival. When plans were being made for the nation's Bicentennial, Fisher suggested some sort of commemorative jar. This was wedded to his earlier idea of reviving the Ideal.

On October 12, 1974, a sample section of a new Ideal, see plate 67, was run in flint in an edition of 75, according to Paul Bredwell, the project manager. Later it was sampled in a color known as "pottery," an opaque creamy milk glass in an edition of 30 jars. All of these were given to officers and directors of the company and to individuals who had worked on the jar.

Plate 65

(Plate 65.) The Ball Eclipse Wide Mouth, in sizes from the half-gallon down to the pint. The two at the left are from the 1920s and the two at the right from the 1930s or later. All have the same "half-moon" lug for bail attachment. The pint has the patent date of July 14, 1908 on the reverse, a rarity for Eclipses.

(Plate 66.) The regular mouth Ball Eclipse in its square version is a close relative of the square Ideal in plate 63. This jar, however, differs in that it has the twisted wire bail. It is a very faint blue, perhaps flint, discolored by the sun.

Plate 66

The production run, begun December 2, 1974, is in Ball blue, and this will be sold commercially in 1975. The bottom of this jar carries the number 75, the year for which it was made.

A limited edition of 5,000, in the same color, which was not intended for sale but to be used as a presentation item, is the same jar with the signature of Edmund F. Ball, the company's former president and board chairman, on the back, across the face of the Bicentennial medallion.

The "Edmund jars" will doubtless get into circulation much more quickly than the two sample-section jars in flint and pottery and may, in years to come, command fancy prices in the collecting market.

There is another side of the Sure Seal-Ideal story, one vitally important to Ball and to jar collectors.

The company had entered the container business in 1880 with its wood-jacketed metal kerosene can. Then it switched, in 1882, to a tin-jacketed glass kerosene can, called the Diamond, made until 1893. Then later, others called the Dandy, the Crown and the Boss were made, into the nineteen-teens.

(Plate 67.) The newest Ball jars — the Ideal Bicentennial issue for 1975.
At left is "the Edmund jar," with Mr. Edmund F. Ball's signature.
Mr. Ball was president of the company during the post-World War II era, prior to the assumption of that position by Mr. Fisher. The second jar is the regular production jar. Third is a sample section, run in an edition of 30 in "pottery," an opaque creamy milkglass. Fourth is a flint sample section, run in an edition of 75 jars. This entire project was supervised by Paul J. Bredwell. Twenty-five of the opaque jars were accidentally broken later.

(Plate 68.) A sample of all of the different types of jars and bottles made by Ball in 1903. Three-L Ball fruit jars are at right on the upper row, just to the right of the mustard jar, designed by George A. Ball for French's.

Ball made some fruit jars, reportedly just a few in 1884 with the bulk of the Buffalo production beginning June 8, 1885 — when the Mason Improved jars were made with glass tops and metal rings, followed quickly by jars with zinc caps — and in 1886 and 1887 until the famous fire.

In the container business, fruit jars dominated production and sales for many decades to follow, although early diversification found Ball to be the first fruit jar company to make and sell jars and fittings together. They made their own zinc caps, then their own wooden shipping crates and then corrugated shipping containers and rubber jar rings. Ball conducted extensive testing before railroads would accept its glass jars for shipment in corrugated paper cartons. This "first" revolutionized rail shipment of products.

Ball was an early entrant into the commercial packerware glass business which evolved into today's position as an important supplier of commercial glass to major food and beverage customers.

In 1903, as plate 68 shows, Ball was making many different types of glass containers, including the French's mustard jar, designed by George A. Ball, and which remained that company's standard jar design for many years. During the Prohibition era Ball made Bevo bottles for Anheuser-Busch, today one of Ball's major customers for its metal containers.

Ball was no stranger to producing glass containers for commercial customers.

There is an interesting series of beautiful jars, almost all of which are wire-bail, glass-top containers, which Ball made from 1908 until the 1930s or 1940s.

Some were for merchants, some were for food packers, and some were for persons or institutions unknown. They can be identified as Ball-made by Ball claims or by the Ball "look". A competitor-firm was also making commercial jars during the

(*Plate 69.*) The Ball-made Chef jar, with the famous patent date, is at left. Without the Chef medallion it would be an exact copy of thousands of Ideal jars. At right is another Chef jar of about the same time made by a Ball competitor. In almost every case where a wire-bail "product" jar shows up it was one made by Ball or the other company and can be identified by such a comparison as this — ignoring, of course, everything on the jar and concentrating on the appearance of the jar.

(*Plate 70.*) The Amazon Swift Seal. Made for an unknown customer in Ball blue. Note the circle or "ball" into which the lettering was placed. This becomes a hallmark of this series of "product" or "customer" jars.

Plate 69

Plate 70

Plate 71

Plate 72

Plate 73

(Plate 71.) Decker's Iowana jar. Made for the Mason City, Iowa meat packer. Again the "ball" device for plate change in the mold.

(Plate 72.) Kohrs of Davenport. Another jar for another Iowa customer.

(Plate 73.) The Lustre, a private-label jar made for a Philadelphia company and like the Kohrs, this jar has never before been attributed to Ball, although it obviously is a Ball jar.

period, sometimes for the same customers, but their jars always looked different from Ball's. See plate 69.

In alphabetical order, for no better reason, some of these commercial jars are:

Amazon Swift Seal, 1910-1920, in quart and pint. (Never before attributed to Ball, but obviously Ball.) See plate 70.

Banner Trademark Warranted WM, and *Banner Trademark Wide Mouth*, 1920-1940, in pint and half-pint, for Fisher-Bruce Co., Philadelphia. (Jar in plate 71 has July 14, 1908 patent date on reverse.)

Chef Trade Mark The Berdan Co., 1930, in quart, for the Berdan Co., Toledo, Ohio. (Jar on left in plate 69 is a Ball jar, bearing the patent date. The jar on the right is an earlier product jar made by a competitor company for Berdan and shows the difference between Ball-made product jars and others.)

Climax Trade Mark Registered U S Pat Off, 1910-1930, also made in flint, for Fisher-Bruce Co., Philadelphia. (Both jars carry the 1908 date.)

Decker's Iowana Mason City, Iowa, 1930, in quart and pint, for Decker's Dependable Foods, Mason City, Iowa. (The patent date is on the reverse of the pint in plate 71 and the brown mark is a label attached to the jar by Ball for its museum indicating its origin. Decker's was a meat packer.)

(Julian Toulouse also reports Ball made the *Decker Dependable Food* jar with a Mason shoulder seal and the *Decker's Victor Mason City, Iowa* jar with a wire bail. The latter has the characteristic circle seen on so many of these jars. Examples of neither could be found for this work.)

Kohrs Davenport, Ia., 1930, in quart. (Patent date on the obverse. This jar has seldom before been attributed to Ball but is obviously from the Ball factories.)

THE LIQUID The Liquid (in diamond in script) *CARBONIC COMPANY.* (For soda pop carbonation).

Lustre R. E. Tongue & Bros. Co. Inc. Phila., in quart and Ball blue, made for the R. E. Tongue & Bros. Co., Inc., Philadelphia, about 1930. (This jar, with the patent date, has not been attributed to Ball previously. Toulouse mentions it, in the wire-bail version, as being found only in flint.) Plate 73.

McDonald New Perfect Seal and *McDonald Perfect Seal*, 1925 and 1920, in half-gallon and quart. (Creswick and Arleta Rodrigues

(Plate 74.) The Quick Seal series, made for Woolworth's, in flint and Ball blue. Note, however, the difference in the bails of the two pints·

(Plate 75.) The Selco Surety Seal, in a half-gallon. Everything about this jar proves its maker to have been Ball.

Plate 74

Plate 75

Plate 76

Plate 77

(*Plate 76.*) The Sure Seal reappears without the Ball name
but as a Ball-made jar in three sizes (half-gallon and pint only shown here)
for L. Bamberger & Co., the Newark, N. J., department store.

(*Plate 77.*) The Tight Seal, made for Kresge stores in at least two sizes.
The jar at left is an aqua-green and the one at right is Ball blue although it was
photographed with a flint lid as it was found in the Ball Museum.

in *Fruit Jars* attribute these jars to Ball although Toulouse says
"maker unknown.")

Quick Seal, 1930-1940, in quart and pint, in flint and aqua,
made by Ball for Woolworth's, some of whose stores are now
called Woolco. (Jar, at right in plate 74, could date back to
1910-1915 period from the appearance of its bail.)

The Rath Packing Co. Waterloo, Iowa, 1920-1930, for Rath Packing Co., for their meats. (The patent date again shows up here.)

Safe Seal, 1920-1935, in Ball blue, in quart. For whom it was
made is unknown. (The patent date, as well as the Toulouse,
Creswick and Rodrigues verifications, indicate this as Ball-
made.)

Selco Surety Seal, 1930-35, in half-gallon and perhaps quart.
Probably made for M. Seller & Co., Portland, Oregon. (Entire
appearance of jar and the patent date, again, prove the jar to
have been Ball-made.) Plate 75.

Sure Seal Made for L. Bamberger & Co., 1918, in half-gallon, quart and pint, made for the Newark, New Jersey, department store. (One of the earliest proliferations of the Sure Seal name, and perhaps used for Bamberger's after the Sure Seal was dropped from the regular Ball line in favor of the Ideal.) Plate 76.

Tight Seal, 1910-1920, in quart and pint, in flint, aqua, and Ball blue. Made for S. S. Kresge Co. some of whose stores are now known as K-Marts. (Patent dates are visible in plate 77 on both jars. Jar on right carries Kresge information from Ball Museum.)

One other jar should be reported here as Ball-made. That is the Acme. This is a wire-bail jar, seen by the author in the Ball Museum in a pint size flint, and is basically square. The embossed frame on the jar front is squared on the lower three sides and arched on top. Inside is a shield with three stars over the word ACME which rises horizontally to the right. A notation on the back of the jar indicates that it was made by

(Plates 78-79.) The Ball Universal, a mysterious jar, was made prior to World War II and may have been in the Ball line for a very short time. At left it is shown with a zinc cap and rubber ring. At right it is shown with a glass lid and would have required a rubber ring for sealing. It would also accommodate the modern two-piece Ball dome lid or the earlier metal ring, glass lid and rubber gasket sealing system.

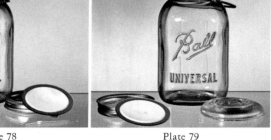

Plate 78   Plate 79

Schram and then Ball after Schram's operations were purchased in 1925.

Only one other jar belongs in this section — the second most enigmatic jar Ball has ever produced. Perhaps it is the best possible bridge to the jars to be discussed next, for it does what no other jar has ever been made to do — accept a glass lid with its wire bail and also accept a conventional zinc screw cap, two-piece tinplated lid, or the old Ball zinc band and No. 10 glass lid.

This is the Ball Universal. Conversations with several people at Ball point to this jar having been made in about 1937 or 1938 as a sample. It was designed by Walter R. Sterrett, the company's long-time chief of mold making and designing. Ball President John W. Fisher estimates probably no more than 50 of the jars were ever made and even fewer fitted with bails.

The base of this jar carries the legend — PATENT APPLIED FOR — in tiny, faint letters.

The only one known is in the Ball Museum and goes virtually unnoticed until attention is called to its top. (See plates 78-79 for the Universal used with different lids.)

The jar fits so well between the Ideal and the Perfect Mason, plate 80, that it is perfectly ideal or ideally perfect. "Well, it certainly is universal," Edmund F. Ball commented about it.

(Plate 80.) For comparison purposes the Universal is a hybrid of the Perfect Mason and the Ideal.

(Plate 81.)

Normalcy and Then Depression . . .
America's '20s and '30s were marked by startling contrasts —
abundance and hope; then shortages and despair.
It was a time when
coffee was ground at home by hand
and fresh eggs came from under the hens, not from a store carton.
Crocks were used for pickles and kraut.
Billy Sunday was a household discussion subject.
Ball exhibited at the Century of Progress, the Chicago World's Fair in 1933,
and gave away salt and pepper shakers
which were miniatures of their famous jars.
Blue Ideals, flint Eclipses, blue, amber and flint Perfect Masons were
being made, first with a smooth outer finish and then with the famous
ribbed grippers. It was a time for saving even pennies,
Bible reading, home entertainment — including reading books and
newspapers and even listening to the new radios,
including the Ball Brothers program on the NBC network on 16 stations.
The brick in this photograph,
used as a bookend is from the old sidewalk in front of the
Huntington, Indiana, Herald-Press, and was given the author by
James and Corrine Quayle.

V

Mason Wasn't Perfect

From about 1895 to about 1910 Ball made a jar called the Ball Mason. It was the standard (not to be confused with the Standard, the wax sealer jar, manufactured from 1888 to 1912) of the line.

Millions upon millions were made in aqua, green, apple green, Ball blue, and flint. Some of the flints can be found today in a dozen hues of lavender, smoky gray, smoky brown, pink and light honey amber.

"There is a difference in the Mason Fruit Jars made by the various manufacturers.

" 'BALL MASON' Fruit Jars are the best because they are made of the best materials, by skilled workmen. The jars are carefully selected, provided with perfect Caps and good Rubbers. They are thoroughly reliable and will keep fruit for years."

That's part of the copy of a little advertisement for Ball Mason Fruit Jars in the August, 1904, issue of "Woman's Home Companion". The ad signed off with "Demand 'BALL MASON' Jars. BALL BROS. GLASS MFG. CO., MUNCIE, IND. Largest Fruit Jar Mfrs. in the World."

The ad writer and the company were not exaggerating. The company had become the largest in the world and the Ball Mason was the best on the market — but it still wasn't perfect.

Ball wanted perfection — and it achieved it with the Perfect Mason but probably not with the Perfection or the Improved.

(*Plate 82.*) The progression from the offset Perfect Mason (the Perfect to the right of the Mason) to the Perfection (with the dropped "R") to the Improved. These three jars were made from apparently identical molds. The Perfection here has a ghost of the Perfect Mason behind it. The Improved is embossed on a plate cut into the Perfection mold. Although the photograph does not show it, close examination of any jars with this type of embossing may reveal a rare series of jars. These belong to Dick Roller who first "uncovered" this riddle.

(*Plate 83.*) Some of the Perfections carried patent dates. At right this one carries two. What the second date means is guesswork for collectors. Note here, too, the similarity of the Ball script between the Perfect Mason (whose FE and S are filling up in the mold) and the Perfection.

(*Plate 84.*) The proper lid for the Perfection is this one with the zinc band and glass insert with a single patent date, one assigned to Ball. The base of the pint jar, shown at right, carries both patent dates.

Plate 82

Plate 83

Plate 84

Ball Perfect Masons exist with the embossing in plain or sans-serif Roman and Italic letters. Toulouse attributes these jars to 1900 to 1915. They are remakes of later vintage Boyd Perfect Mason molds as is shown in plates 39-40.

The advent of the Owens machine allowed the development of this jar which is still in the line and in fact is the basic line of Ball today, although the word "Perfect" has disappeared from the regular-mouth Ball Mason and even the word "Mason" has disappeared from the Ball Wide Mouth jar of today.

The ground lip and shoulder seal were gone for practical purposes. A top seal was now possible.

However, the famous Perfect Mason appeared first in edition E of *The Ball Canning & Preserving Recipes*, published in 1914. The Perfect Mason name is used in late 1913 in edition C over a drawing of a Mason jar.

About the Perfect Mason, edition F in 1915 states, "With Zinc Porcelain Lined Caps. The standard of all Jars. This jar has acquired its good name (a modest enough claim) and popularity by its real superiority over other jars. (The word "real" is the key. Ball had achieved its major breakthrough.) So well known that no details are necessary except that it is made by a new process which is told of in this book. Read it."

I did.

Page 36 of the book describes the Owens machine and pictures it. One paragraph of the copy is appropriate to quote: ". . . this insures that the Jars and trimmings being made under one management will be more perfect fitting than could be expected where the glass is produced by one maker, and the metal or some other parts by other makers, neither being able to know just what is necessary to make his product fit the product of the other." Well put — and it was this self-manufacture of every part of the Ball jar — the jar, the glass liner for the lid, the zinc cap, the rubber, the wire bail for the Sure Seal (Ideal), the screwbands for the Improved jars and the glass lids for this jar — that led Ball to an early state of diversity and independence.

Ball has indicated that it wanted and still wants to be sure that its products meet the needs of the current generation it serves.

Thus we can place the first Ball Perfect Mason in 1913, to be augmented in 1914 with the Perfection which in 1915 was replaced by the Improved.

Before jumping into that, the collector must step back just a bit to the Perfection. In plate 82 one can see the natural progression from Perfect Mason to Perfection to Improved. These

(Plate 85.) Where the Perfection failed, the Improved seemed to flourish as witnessed by this procession of jars in three sizes, two colors and two shapes. All took zinc bands and glass lids. The third jar shows the narrowed opening for the jar which caused some lack of acceptance by consumers. The square blue jar is one of the most handsome in the line.

three jars, when examined closely, are really one and the same in that they came from a common set of molds, reworked twice to achieve the third jar.

Dick Roller's research on this question is of great value. The Perfection in plate 82 has a "ghosted" Perfect scattered through the word Perfection, beginning at the "r" and ending before the "n". Below that is the "ghosting" of Mason.

Roller points out that perhaps having achieved the Perfect Mason, Ball wanted the Perfection with a glass top held in place by a metal screw band, the same kind of glass-rubber-glass seal obtained already by the wire-bail Sure Seal (which is described in a 1913 *Blue Book* as "perfect").

The Perfection carries two patent dates. See plate 83. The April 10, 1900, date patent was assigned to Ball. However, the second date of April 26, 1907, is a mystery. The pints carry the patent dates on the base and the jars take an embossed lid. See plate 84. The lid is the only known piece of fruit jar glass ever to carry the mention of Muncie. This jar is also known in half-pints.

Roller's third jar in plate 82 shows a mold plate inserted where Perfection-Perfect Mason had been and with the word

Improved dropped in. Later Improved jars do not show this plate remake.

Ball President John Fisher says the Perfection was too expensive to make and that the zinc band distorted in processing food.

Roller points out that the Perfection did not have the same size mouth as the Perfect Mason zinc top jars and that the early Improved jars had the same "fault." This was later modified when zinc "went to war" in 1941-1945 and the glass top No. 10 and V glass lids with tinplate bands came along.

Zinc bands were used for many years as the second piece of the two-piece closure, even with the tinplate Vacu-Seal lid. World War II's shortage of zinc forced conversion completely to the tinplate band known so well today.

The glass top, screw band jar continued in the line for a number of years, with the bulk of the Improved production going, after World War I, to the export market until the jar was discontinued in 1922.

The Improved came in sizes from half-gallon down to pint (although that is not shown in this book). This jar was also made in flint and Ball blue and in round and square configurations.

The second jar, from left, in plate 85 carries the legend "Made in U.S.A." Its Ball script is also bereft of the famous underscore — which seemed to be a hallmark of the jars of the '20s. I believe this to have been one destined for export.

Some of the script on the Ball Improved series seems to have been produced from molds identical and perhaps concurrent with

(*Plate 86.*) A "plain" Ball and a Ball Improved. The style of the script embossing would indicate a common "birth date" for these two jars, between 1913 and 1922.

molds used to make jars marked only with the Ball in script. See plate 86.

"Plain" Ball jars, as these are sometimes called, pop up repeatedly in various eras.

There is one, plate 44, which is embossed with Ball with the underscore making a third "L". It has been overlooked often in the Ball Museum. Plate 44 shows its uniqueness. It has a tin-plate cap with interrupted threads and a thin rubber gasket for shoulder sealing although it has a beaded lip. A test jar when the Owens machine was new?

The ABGA Mason Perfect Made in U.S.A. has long confused collectors, who have speculated as to its maker and the meaning of the initials.

It is Ball blue as plate 87 shows clearly. The lettering of Mason Perfect is nearly identical to Ball's Perfect Mason lettering. It has an Improved closure — embossed glass top (as does the Improved) and a zinc screw band — and no other company was making such a jar about that time. Ball was exporting the Improved in the years 1918-1922.

(Plate 87.) Another relative of both the Perfect Mason and the Improved is the ABGA Mason Perfect, long one of the most enigmatic jars collectors have encountered. Compare it first, in color and finish, to Perfect Mason at the left. Then compare the neck and mouth to the Improved at the right. Note also the peculiar formation of the small "a" in Ball on both jars and the apparent capital "A" on the ABGA. This jar took a zinc ring and glass lid, also embossed as had been the Perfection lid in plate 84. Jar collectors have a difficult time sorting some of these mysteries. The best guide, in the absence of written evidence (and there are varying degrees of evidence), is looking at and handling a jar and comparing it with others.

Finally, after much speculation and research it has now been determined that Ball did, indeed, make these jars. They were for the Anglo-Belge Glass Association of London, England, and were made from approximately 1918 to 1924. How so many of them have been found in the United States and Canada by collectors is still unknown.

It was not until 1934 that Ball had a two-piece metal closure for its Perfect Mason. The Vacu-Seal lids later gave way to the more-famous Dome lids with the ping sound when they seal which proved to be an excellent selling point for the lids.

Refinement of the Perfect Mason did not stand still. It was produced in half-gallon, quart, pint and half-pint and even in miniatures (as salesmen's samples). These miniatures led to the development of at least four distinct versions of salt and pepper shakers, the first offered at the 1933 Century of Progress, as the Chicago World's Fair was officially known.

The Perfect Masons were produced in flint and Ball blue through the 1920s and 1930s until the blue was phased out in 1937 along with all other blue glass.

There are numerous examples (and unfortunately the photographs I have seen are not reproducible) of a Perfect Mason in what is sometimes called the three pint or the quart-and-a-half. Some of them measure down as small as 42 ounces.

It is claimed that these "short half-gallons" were eagerly sought by bootleggers in certain areas in the late '20s and early

(*Plate 88.*) An amber Perfect Mason, from the 1930s, probably made to go inside an insulated water or beverage container. The jar at the right is a 1920s flint, filled with summer squash in the 1940s and still in excellent condition, ready to eat.

BALL BROTHERS COMPANY
RADIO PROGRAM - "CANNING TIME"

JUNE 22ND TO OCTOBER 4TH 1931
STANDARD TIME OF THE CITY NAMED - - ALL DAY TIME HOURS

STATIONS		MON.	TUES.	WED.	THURS.	FRI.
WORCESTER	WORC			11:15		11:15
SCHENECTADY	WGY				12:15	12:15
CINCINNATI	WLW	8:15		8:15		
ATLANTA	WSB			8:45		8:45
CHICAGO	WLS		1:00			1:00
ST. LOUIS	KWK	11:15			11:15	
ST. PAUL	KSTP	12:30		12:30		
TOPEKA	WIBW			11:15		11:15
FORT WORTH	WBAP	9:45			9:45	
DENVER	KOA	11:30		1:00		
SALT LAKE	KSL			7:00		7:00
SPOKANE	KHQ			10:00		10:00
SEATTLE	KJR		10:15		10:15	
PORTLAND	KGW		9:45			9:45
SAN FRANCISCO	KPO		10:15			10:15
LOS ANGELES	KNX	11:00		11:00		

Plate 89

'30s while Prohibition was still in force. The 42-ounce jar allowed more "half-gallons" of moonshine to be filled from one still.

Other companies already made square jars, sought by bootleggers because they could carry more of them in the space they had if the jars were square.

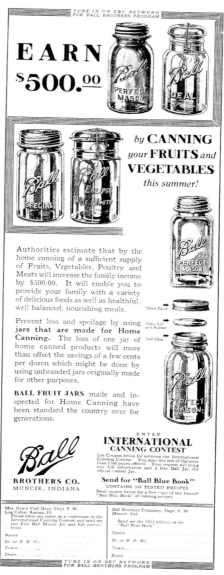

(*Plate 90.*) An advertisement from the August 1932 issue of "The Farmer's Wife."

Plate 91   Plate 92

(Plate 91.) Two of the later Specials, the quart from the late 1920s and the other from the 1930s after the gripper marks were added.

(Plate 92.) An early Special in a half-pint size — a very squat, dumpy jar and very collectible, especially in Ball blue, shown here at its best.

From the mid-'20s through the '30s and into the early '40s Ball made a square Perfect Mason as well as a round Perfect Mason. Some modifications to the bottom of the square and round jars were made in the '30s. However, with the advent of World War II and the formation of the War Production Board, both shapes were discarded for a single shape which embodied both designs and saved mold metal, giving America's house-wives the round-square of today, a jar which fits more conveniently on the pantry shelf and on the collector's shelf — too.

Most other jar manufacturers adopted the new Ball shape for their jars because of the success of the new style.

Ball made Perfect Masons in amber and flint in the early 1930s and late 1940s, apparently not for canning but for sale to companies making water jugs which needed a glass container to put inside the insulation.

Later, other Perfect Masons, in a deeper amber, were made at Ball's Hillsboro, Illinois, plant between 1956 and 1961 when the operation there was closed. (Ball made amber pharmaceutical, whiskey and beer bottles at Hillsboro.) All of these jars were tests for a new machine, according to John Fisher. Plate 94 shows the half-gallon and the pint. Whether a quart was made

I do not know. An elderly woman in Oklahoma wrote Ball last year saying she had found a half-gallon in an abandoned cow pasture near her home, some 15 years after it was lost.

Toulouse puts the Ball Special, a wide-mouth version of the Perfect Mason, into circulation to the absence of the underscore on the script, I would place in the late 1920s. See plate 91. The other jar in the plate has the gripper marks, so it is obviously later. The Ball blue Special pint is one of the most collectible of this series. Plate 92. A Special of some sort, with a shoulder seal, was made between 1913 and 1920 according to a company sales flyer printed after the Greenfield purchase.

In the 1940s and 1950s, the Special had the words Wide Mouth added to the front. It was only a few small steps to take Special off and leave it Ball Wide Mouth as it is today.

An interesting sidelight to the Ball Special series is shown in plate 98. In 1936, Fred J. Petty, then general sales manager and a son-in-law of President Frank C. Ball, received the jar and lid on the right from the Pacific Commercial Company in New York which had received it from its Manila office. It is a Japanese copy of the Ball Special — down to the embossing on the front and sides of the jar and on the zinc cap — in Spanish and

(*Plate 93.*) The specials of post-World War II look like the Perfect Masons of that time.

Plate 94

Plate 95

Plate 96

Plate 97

(Plate 94.) Two ambers and two flints in the post-Korean War era.
The ambers were made at Ball's Hillsboro, Ill., glass plant.

(Plate 95.) The first and third lines of Ball freezer jars.
The two at right were developed immediately after World War II.
Those at the left came into the line in the mid- to late-fifties.
The second jar from left was in general use as a medical specimen jar at Ball
Memorial Hospital in Muncie in 1959 when the author received it,
containing his gallstones, from the nurse who later became his wife.
It was the first jar in his collection — and the most treasured.

(Plate 96.) The intermediate freezer jar is second from right.
It shows all of the embossing, including the Ball script and the grippers with
a stippled finish. The container at left is a Ball-designed and made jug,
probably for syrup, manufactured in 1900.
The second jar is a poor-quality "St. Johnsbury" Sure Seal (see text).
Note the off-center hemispherical lugs for the bail, which is missing.
This was used for maple syrup. The jar at right is a jar which was marketed in
the 1950s and was used in a children's jelly making kit about that time.
It took a No. 63 two-piece lid. Many people found it excellent for left-overs.

(Plate 97.) The Strittmatter's honey bee jar, a special-order jar made in
pints only. This is one of the most delightful of all Ball-made jars.

(Plate 98.) The Ball Special Made in U.S.A. (perhaps an export jar)
and the Bola Especial. Ball did not make the jar and lid at the right.
It was made in Japan in the 1930s for export to the Philippines.
Note the copy of the grip marks, the style of script, the underscore.
The jar on the left, chosen initially to illustrate the copy of a Ball jar,
is historic in its own right. It was dropped from an airplane over Muncie in 1939
and survived with only the glass liner of the cap breaking. These milkglass
fragments can be seen in the bottom of the jar near the yellow label.

Plate 98

it was being exported by a Japanese trading company to the Philippines, a Spanish-speaking nation, still then controlled by the United States. In fact, a Hoosier, former Governor Paul V. McNutt, was governor-general of the Philippines at the time. The price of the jar, net, was 87 cents a dozen. Ball's was $1.02 at the time.

The jar in the same plate, on the left, was dropped from an endurance airplane, "Miss Suntan", flying at 60 miles per hour at an altitude of 100 feet over the Muncie Airport on September 14, 1939. The only thing broken was the porcelain liner of the cap — another tribute to the strength of Ball-made glass.

One more jar, in the Perfect Mason series, merits attention at this point. It is the Strittmatter's Pure Honey Put Up By F. J. Strittmatter & Wife R. D. 1 Ebenburg, Pa. It was made in a pint only. (See plate 97.)

This jar, a private "label" made in the 1920s by Ball, is one of the most attractive jars in the entire Ball Museum collection. Although relatively rare, it commands a low price in the collector's price guides — perhaps because of some collectors' fin-

(*Plates 99-100-101.*) In the '20s the Perfect Mason had taken on a clean square shape, left photo. Walter Sterrett relates that in the early '30s some of the jars were breaking after processing and that F. C. Ball asked him to redesign the jar. Center photograph shows a 1934 jar with the rounded bottom to put more strength in this area which had caused difficulty. This jar also was the first to use the two-piece Vacu-Seal lid, as the note on the reverse indicates. At right is the next development with still another change in the script. The long hook on the ascender of the "B" is shortened and the loop in the "B" is eliminated. The underscore stays closer to the letters as it descends.

| Plate 99 | Plate 100 | Plate 101 |

ickiness about "product" jars. To overlook this one is to miss a real beauty in glass.

After World War II, home canners had something new in the way of preserving food. Jar makers had new competition coming down the pike. And commercial food producers had new competition for their glass and tin canned foods. The freezer and frozen food had arrived.

Spotting its opportunity early, Ball had its chief mold designer, Walter Sterrett, with Fred Dellwo, manager of the packaging and processing research department, work on new freezer containers for frozen food.

They developed a line of containers which is a fine descendent of the Perfect Mason.

The tapered shape permitted easy removal of contents from a jar in a frozen state. Wide-mouth caps were developed, see plate 95, so that the jars would stack or nest one on the other — first in the locker plants which sprang up across the country and later in the home freezers. It could be stacked top-to-top and bottom-to-bottom to save freezer space.

The first jar was called Ball Freezer Jar. The next generation was Ball Refrigerator and Freezer Jar, capitalizing on the use

(*Plates 102-103-104.*) Cups and ounces measurements came onto the jar in the late 1950s, left photo. The sculptured fruit medallion was added in the early 1960s, first at the El Monte plant, center photo. Today's regular jar looks like this with still more modification of the script — and the word Perfect is gone.

| Plate 102 | Plate 103 | Plate 104 |

(Plate 105.) In 1974 Ball became the first fruit jar maker in the world
to mark its jars with metric graduations, shown here in the
400 milliliter (pint) and 800 milliliter (regular and wide-mouth quart) sizes.
These will become standard in 1975.

of home freezers in service by that time. Finally that all was
dropped in favor of a similar tapered jar — this time without
grippers, but with measurements — which was called Ball. Now
these have been modified to put the sculptured fruit medallion
on the reverse — the same medallion promoted by Ball's West
Coast sales manager Phill Goetz in 1962. Goetz was similarly
responsible for the Quilted Crystal jelly glasses which took the
homemaker's fancy.

For a while the sculptured glass jar was made only at the
El Monte, California, plant starting in 1962. A few jars filtered
east and commanded high prices until collectors found out about
them and passed the word to the unsuspecting. Today the fruit
medallion is the standard on the reverse of the Ball Mason and
Ball Wide Mouth as well as on the Freezer or Tapered jars. A
new series of decorated lids came along to capture the homemaker's fancy.

Cups and ounces measurements were added in 1956 to the side
of the jar, an idea of Russell Simpson. In 1974 metric marks
were placed on the left side of the jar, as a result of an idea by
Howard Jones, Mary Lou Williamson and James Sproat. The
Mundelein, Illinois, plant made the first of these in the quart
Ball Mason. Later in the year the Asheville, North Carolina,
plant, according to Manager Bill Doud, made the metric jar
in the Wide Mouth quart and the Mason pint. These jars will

Plate 106   Plate 107

(*Plate 106.*) Blue Perfect Masons were made from 1915 until 1937
with various modifications. This one, a half-pint, is from the early 1930s.
The little jar at right was never meant for canning.
It is a miniature of the square jar (the square and the round were companion
jars for many years) and was a salesman's sample. The zinc cap
did not have perforations in it and the jar came with a rubber ring.
This little jar spawned the salt and pepper shaker series.

(*Plate 107.*) Today's companion to the regular mouth Mason is the
Ball Wide Mouth, the descendant of the Special. It is shown here with a worn
mold, similar to one in which it was formed.

(*Plate 108.*) Caps and lids of all sizes and descriptions.
The cobalt blue lid was a limited, hand-made souvenir for Ball shareholders
about five years ago. It fits a wide-mouth Eclipse jar. The Ball V was
a wartime lid as was the No. 10. Ball switched to these lids to help save zinc
for shell casings in the war effort.

be the standard line for Ball in 1975, making Ball the first company in the world to mark its fruit jars with metric measurements as well as the traditional cups and ounces.

In 1974 Ball repeatedly announced to the consuming public that it was making all jars and fittings at planned capacity. The company never caught up with the demand which had been building for several months but which peaked in 1974 and promises to go higher in 1975. Never before had Ball produced so many jars. Conservative estimates would put the company's entire production over the past 90 years in excess of four billion jars.

Today the jars retail to the housewife something on the order of 20 cents each. In 1896 the cost was 12 cents each to the consumer and down to 5 cents each in 1897.

It's little wonder then that home canning has remained popular and is still a conservative, economical, uncomplicated, creative and nutritious adjunct to feed a family.

Ball succeeded in making Mr. Mason's idea not only perfect, but ideal.

(Plate 109.) A parade of salt and pepper shakers, including an original set and box used at the Chicago World's Fair. The second set was in the '40s with the two colors of lids. The third pair are from the '50s and differ only in the size of holes in the lids. The current set, shown with their container, show the removal of the word "Perfect" and blue and white lids.

(Plate 110.)
4-H Clubs are so much a part of American life
that they are no longer a rural activity.
But in the pre- and post-World War II times much 4-H work
revolved around gardening and the County Fair.
This display, viewed through an old kitchen window,
shows an amber Ball half-gallon, a quart of tomato pickles,
a pint of cider jelly, an aqua quart of black-eyed peas,
a pint of dilly beans and a quart of tomatoes.
The black and white photographs are of
actual 4-H and County Fair scenes from Muncie and Delaware County.
The old license plate, usually found nailed to the side of a barn,
is from North Carolina in 1933.

VI

Rummage Relish

The current *Blue Book* contains a recipe for Rummage Relish, made with green tomatoes, ripe tomatoes, cabbage, onions, celery, green peppers, sweet red peppers, cucumbers and a host of spices, sugar, salt and vinegar. It does make a tasty relish and seems to use every possible leftover from the garden.

This chapter is a collection of rummage which may be relished by the collector.

✳ ✳ ✳

In the early days, Ball jars were stored in Muncie fields south of what is now Memorial Drive. Millions of jars would be stacked out in the fields with straw separating them. Flocks of migrating ducks heading south in the fall of the year spotted the shimmering fields and several landed — obviously thinking it was a nice lake. Stories, perhaps apocryphal, are told of the difficulties of first getting the ducks off the jars and then getting the jars cleaned.

✳ ✳ ✳

Speaking of the *Blue Book*, it went through several title changes over the years.

(*Plate III.*) A man stands atop a sea of glass jars in the fields south of Muncie's glass plants where jars were stored between layers of straw until ready for shipment. The photograph was made sometime in 1903.

The first title was *The Correct Method for Preserving Fruit.* In 1913 the edition merely made the word Method plural. The next edition, also in 1913, dropped the word The from the title and the cover carried the first photograph — in color — of peaches on a tree.

The next edition dropped the color photograph and substituted a new title, *The Ball Preserving Book,* the first time Ball's name appeared in the title.

In 1914 the title was the same but the cover was a nicely embossed design with Sure Seal and Mason jars illustrated — Sure Seal getting the top position!

The Ball Mason jar appeared as the only illustration on the cover of the next edition which was called *The Ball Canning & Preserving Recipes.* This was edition E in 1914 also and the center spread pictured the Ball Perfect Mason, filled with cherries,

Plate 112   Plate 113

(*Plates 112-113*). This souvenir Ball Bros Glass Mfg Co. Muncie. Ind.
plate was apparently made about 1910. It is one of the best of all Ball
"go-withs" and is extremely rare. The plate at the right, for
The Premium Glass Co Coffeyville Kan, appears to have been made at the same
time and by the same glassmaker. It is possible Ball and Premium could
have used the same supplier or perhaps Ball made both of them.
These two plates supply some foundation for the speculation that Ball
purchased Premium. It could, however, have been mere coincidence.

(*Plate 114.*) Blue Books from 1911 to 1974.
The first two are 1911 and 1913. The third one is from the 1930s and
the fourth is 1974's edition. In front of them is a 1930 Ideal jar, once owned by
the author's wife's grandmother, Birgie May McKinley Miller,
filled with dilly beans. The other jar, a Quilted Crystal jelly glass,
contains Bordeaux jelly.

in full color. The word Perfect was offset to the right of the word Mason which appeared directly below the Ball script.

A printed simulation of brown leather was featured on the cover of edition F in 1915 and showed the Ball Perfect Mason with the latter two words centered under the script. The title was *The Ball Canning and Preserving Receipts*. Note the change from recipes to receipts. The back of this one featured the Ball Improved jar.

In edition G, issued in July 1915, we first find the famous words "Blue Book". The cover was two colors of blue and it was called *The Ball Blue Book of Canning and Preserving Receipts*.

Two editions later, in 1916, the name was the same but the cover had an illustration of a jar marked only with the under-

(*Plate 115.*) Ball jelly glasses, while not technically qualifying as fruit jars, are interesting kinds of "go-withs." Here one is shown used as a candle holder. This one was made by a four-year-old in 1973 for his father's collection at Christmas.

(*Plate 116.*) Letters by the millions pour into Ball offices.
This envelope, saved because of its multiple addresses —
mailed to Muncie, Hillsboro, Huntington, Sapulpa, and Wichita Falls —
contained a request for a Blue Book, most likely.
The brass letter opener, a fine "go-with" is owned by Vern C. Schranz,
Ball's corporate secretary. The silver-plate opener, shorter but of the same
style, is owned by Norman Barnett, a Flat Rock, Ind., collector.
The letter was mailed Aug. 31, 1929 from Iron River, Mich.

(*Plate 117.*) One of the interesting and humorous letters received by the thousands each year about home canning. The Nebraska lady
was having a problem with the early confusion over vitamins.
She probably had canned millions of vitamins without knowing it.
The notation in the upper left of the letter indicates she was sent the help she asked.

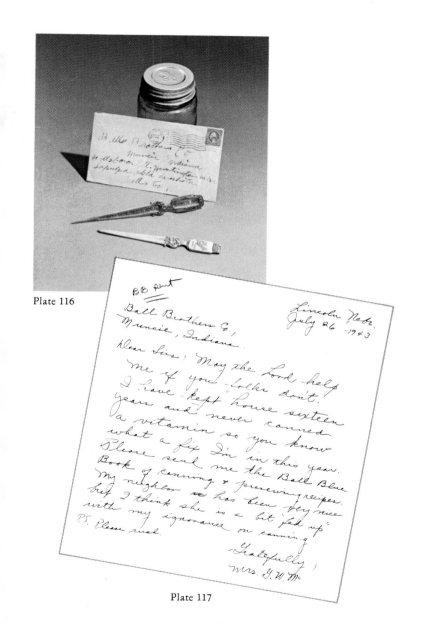

Plate 116

Plate 117

Plate 118　　　　　　　　　Plate 119

Plate 120

Plate 122

Plate 121

(*Plates 118-119-120-121-122.*)
The wooden box end, top, is one of the earliest known to have been made by Ball. Although the company began its packaging revolution by packing in a dozen quantity in 1894, this example probably dates to 1895. Second from top: This pint box end shows the slanting script and the word Mason on the jar illustration, making it a little later. Upper right: This version, for half-gallons, shows only the word Ball in underscored script. Note the peculiar "Trade Mark" of intertwined letters in a circle or "ball" on each of these box ends. It is presumed this means "Ball Brothers," although no record of a trade mark registration has been found.
Bottom left: One of the first corrugated paper boxes, first used by Ball in the early 1900s for shipping jars. Bottom right: This carton, while not of the historic significance of those above, is interesting for its use of script for Ideal, which never appeared on a jar that way, for the off-and-on use of the underscore with the name, for the use of the word "Perfect" on the upper flap, and for the "typo" in the spelling of Owens name.

scored script. Perhaps this is the date of these ''plain'' Ball jars.

Edition K, date not determined, changed the name by dropping the word Receipts. Edition L, date again not determined, changed it again by adding the word Recipes.

There it stayed until 1930 when the title became *The Ball Blue Book*, never again to be substantially changed although today's book is known without the word The.

✷ ✷ ✷

Wooden cases or barrels had been used to ship jars with Ball pioneering the use of wooden cases which would hold six dozen pints, eight dozen quarts, and six dozen half-gallons. These were packed with straw for safety of the glass.

Then, in 1894, Ball made its first wooden boxes, of Michigan pine, for shipment of jars in dozen lots to grocers. The jars were protected by strawboard liner-dividers. This packaging innovation was a revolution in the grocery trade.

After the wooden boxes, some of which survive today and are eagerly-sought fruit jar ''go-withs'', Ball pioneered the use of the corrugated paper shipping box for glass containers, about 1902.

The company purchased the Westside Paper Mill of the United Boxboard Company in Muncie in 1916, the American Strawboard Company plant in Noblesville, Indiana, in 1923, and the Eaton, Indiana, Strawboard Mill in 1933.

In 1934 the company purchased the Danville, Illinois, Paper Mill of Cornstalks Products Company. This was an attempt to make paper from hemp. The hemp paper operation did not succeed.

In 1933 the company seriously considered its need for a Southern paper mill. It was making its own paper and board at the time, in line with its long-time policy of integrated manufacturing for all the product.

A site was selected, plans made and capital earmarked. The plant was to have cost $7 million. The site was south of Fernandina, Florida, on Amelia Island. However, the decision was reversed and the company began a gradual withdrawal from the paper business.

✳ ✳ ✳

It is nothing short of ironic that the Consumer Products Division of the Ball Glass Container Group, in November of 1974, chose a new resort on Amelia Island south of Fernandina for its annual sales meeting where plans for 1975 were heard. Probably no one at that meeting realized they were walking and riding over what might have been a Ball paper mill.

✳ ✳ ✳

A subject of errors was mentioned earlier. It is well to note that most of these occur in the wire bail jars with the patent dates. Almost always it is a wrong numeral in 14, 1908 or a backward numeral. "Three-L" jars are not errors.

Two errors, both owned by Mrs. Alice Creswick, which I find of interest are a pint Ball Mason with the embossing upside

(Plate 123.) In 1975 there is a new line of canning "go-withs," here showing a corn cutter, jar lifters and a plastic funnel. The well-known "pyramid" jar opener will be offered in a limited area with the other items which will be sold in grocery stores.

down, and a quart Ball Perfect Mason of solid glass — weighing six pounds with no trace of an inside cavity. The solid glass jar is undoubtedly a glassmaker's trick. With all the checks made on jars before shipment it could have never been shipped for sale.

The upside-down embossing, suggesting a dispenser, is not a bona fide error. Ball made numerous dispenser jars. A famous one was a pint Ball Special made with upside-down embossing for Caterpillar tractor air filters for many years.

At least four other glass plants operated in Muncie and made fruit jars.

The most famous was Hemingray Glass Co., which moved to Muncie in 1888, just east of the Ball site across Macedonia Avenue. There they made not only their world-famous insulators, the collecting of which is a mania all unto itself, but the highly-prized amber Globe fruit jar with its unique cam lever locking device. The flint, aqua, olive and black Globes were also made in Muncie. It is not believed that Hemingray made its other two jars in Muncie. The company never put its name on its jars.

The second which also made fruit jars in Muncie was Port Glass Company which started in 1891 and which moved out when gas began to fail in 1902 to Belleville, Illinois. Ball acquired this company two years later. Port Avenue in Muncie is named either for the founder or for his company. A substantial number of aqua wax sealers marked PORT on the bottom can be found around Muncie. A Port Mason was also made in Muncie. At one time, about 1900, the company was known as Port and Streeter Glass Company.

The Nelson Fruit Jar Co., Muncie, produced a jar called the Safety in aqua and amber from 1893 to 1896 before going out of business.

The fourth was the Muncie Glass Co. about which little is known except that it made beer and beverage bottles. The Boldt Mason Jar was made in Muncie from 1892 until 1912 when the company moved.

Still another company, Turner Brothers Glass Co., reportedly made fruit jars at the turn of the century. They continued in the glass business, but not the fruit jar business, at Cicero, Terre Haute, and Winchester, Indiana, later. The company eventually became part of the Anchor-Hocking merger.

Patterson Glass Co., Yorktown, six miles west of Muncie, also made fruit jars in the gas boom. The one known to collectors is The Leader. Another, but unconfirmed, jar reportedly made there was called the Winner.

Another glass facet to the history of Delaware County, of which Muncie is the county seat, was the Model Flint Glass Company and the Buckeye Window Glass Company, both of Albany, Indiana, about 12 miles northeast of Muncie. The Model organization, in operation from 1893 until 1902, produced a wide and varied line of tableware which is highly prized by collectors of that sort of glass.

Also located in Albany concurrently was the North Baltimore Bottle Glass Company which produced soft drink and beer bottles from 1893 when the gas boom began for the little town until 1902 when it ended. A few examples of Albany bottles are in existence.

A dimension of the gas boom is indicated by an Albany newspaper of the time which indicated the town had 13 saloons, four churches, two hotels and three undertakers.

Fruit jar "go-withs", an emerging area of interest to collectors, include various boxes and cartons, lids, rings, advertising materials included in the selling cartons and in publications, and such items as ashtrays, pencils, pencil clips, spoons, and letter openers.

Other "go-withs" include those items made specifically for use in canning. Ball has made such items as jar lifters, jar openers and at least five kinds of pressure cookers — the Ball, the Ideal, the Eclipse, the Special and the Thrifty. Ball is currently marketing a line of canning "go-withs." These are a jar lifter, a bubble freer, a corn cutter and a canning funnel.

The various editions of the *Blue Book* also qualify as "go-withs."

* * *

How is it possible to can in a jar? Many persons believe the word can is a contraction of the word canister, and that book-keepers, when they were tired of writing the word in their ledgers, shortened it to can.

A jar normally means a wide-mouth glass container as contrasted to a bottle which is a narrow-neck glass container.

Can comes from the Middle English word *canne*, which comes from the Old High German word *channa*. It means a tinplate container or a jar used to preserve food or other products for later use.

Canning became the verb-form of the noun just as today's language gives us the word programming for the action of writing a program for a computer.

"Putting up" food has also aroused its share of curiosity as a term. It is believed to have originated as the housewife finished her canning and then put up her jars on a shelf in a darkened area for later use — thus they were put up. Later it came to be synonymous with the word canning itself. It can be contrasted to another term involving food preservation — laying down or putting down. Meat, when salted or brined or after it was smoked, was laid down. Some vegetables were laid down in brine or put down in the ground, or later in root cellars.

So it has been possible to can in Ball jars, never Ball bottles, or to put things up in them, even after the contents had been laid down. Ball has been — and still is — a good name to put up with.

A canister, on the other hand, is word of Latin origin, a *canistrum*, meaning a basket, which came from the Greek *kanastron* which in turn came from *kanna* which was a reed. The word, thus, means a box or can, probably of reed, for holding a dry product. Later it meant — and still does — the container for containing shot in an artillery shell, a way to keep powder dry.

APPENDIX I
Ball-Made Jars

NOTE: All upper and lower case script is indicated in upper and lower case letters here. All non-script lettering is in capital letters. Underscored names are underscored. The third "L" loop on the Ball name script is indicated with a third L in the name on those jars bearing this distinctive characteristic.

ABGA (script) MASON PERFECT MADE IN U.S.A.

AMAZON SWIFT SEAL

ACME

Ball (shoulder seal)

BALL (reverse) (Star and crescent letter and design on obverse)

BALL BBGMCo (monogram) FRUIT JAR

BALL DELUXE JAR (Pine mold remake)

Ball ECLIPSE

Ball ECLIPSE WIDE MOUTH

Ball HALF-PINT (lower case letters)

Ball FREEZER JAR

Ball IDEAL

Ball IDEAL (Bicentennial medallion on reverse)

Ball IDEAL (Bicentennial medallion and
              Edmund F. Ball signature on reverse)

Ball IDEAL

Ball IDEAL PAT'D JULY 14, 1908

Ball IDEAL PAT'D JULY 14, 1908

Ball IDEAL (obverse) PROPERTY OF SOUTHERN
METHODIST ORPHANS HOME
WACO, TEXAS (reverse)

Ball IMPROVED (straddle lip top seal)

Ball IMPROVED MADE IN U.S.A.
(straddle lip top seal)

Ball MASON (shoulder seal)

Ball MASON (Root mold remake) (shoulder seal)

Ball MASON (beaded seal)

Ball MASON'S PATENT

Ball MASON'S PATENT 1858

Ball MASON'S PATENT (machine made, beaded seal)

Ball MASON'S (Keystone design) PATENT NOV 30TH 1858

Ball MASON'S PATENT NOV 30TH 1858

BALL (reverse) MASON'S PATENT NOV 30TH 1858 (obverse)

Ball (reverse) MASON'S PATENT 1858 (obverse)
(Port mold remake)

BALL MASON'S PATENT NOV 30TH 1858

BALL (reverse) MASON'S PATENT NOV 30TH 1858 (obverse)

Ball PERFECTION

Ball PERFECTION PAT. APR. 10, 1900. APR. 26, 1907.

Ball PERFECT MASON (beaded seal)

Ball PERFECT MASON (beaded seal) (ribbed)

Ball PERFECT MASON (crude remake of Drey mold,
underscore is part of Drey "y")
(MASON offset to right of PERFECT)

BALL (arched) PERFECT MASON (3 lines centered)
(Boyd mold remake) (horizontal of second L
extended to right in exaggerated fashion)

BALL (Italics) PERFECT MASON
(3 lines centered) (Boyd mold remake)

BALL PERFECT MASON (last word italics) (3 lines centered)
(Boyd mold remake)

BALL PERFECT MASON (3 lines centered)
(Boyd mold remake)

BALL PERFECT MASON (3 lines, second and third
progressively indented)
(Boyd mold remake)

Ball PERFECT MASON (beaded seal) (ribbed)

Ball PERFECT MASON (beaded seal) (square)

Ball PERFECT MASON (beaded seal)

Ball PERFECT MASON (debossed script and letters)
(1920 Mason finish)
BALL (on base in circle)

BALL PERFECT MASON (italics) (Boyd mold remake)

Ball PERFECT MASON (double lined script and letters)
(1920 Mason finish) (distinct break
in script between "a" and first "l")

Ball REFRIGERATOR AND FREEZER JAR

Ball SANITARY SURE SEAL

Ball SURE SEAL (third L loop removed with
ghosting remaining)

Ball SANITARY SURE SEAL PAT'D JULY 14, 1908

Ball SPECIAL (beaded seal)

Ball SPECIAL (beaded seal)

Ball SPECIAL WIDE MOUTH MADE IN U.S.A.

Ball SPECIAL WIDE MOUTH (obverse)
MADE IN U.S.A. (reverse)

Ball SQUARE MASON (beaded seal) (remake of Drey mold)

Ball STANDARD (wax sealer)

Ball SURE SEAL

Ball SURE SEAL PACKED IN ST. JOHNSBURY, VT. BY
THE TOWLE MAPLE PRODUCTS CO.

Ball SURE SEAL PAT'D JULY 14, 1908

Ball TAPERED MASON (beaded seal)

Ball THE Mason (shoulder seal)

Ball UNIVERSAL (wire bail, glass top and Mason screw top)

Ball WIDE MOUTH

Balll (shoulder seal)

Balll (interrupted threads, shoulder seal)

Balll IMPROVED (straddle lip top seal)

Balll IMPROVED (shoulder seal)

Balll IMPROVED MASON (straddle lip top seal)

Balll IMPROVED MASONS PATENT 1858 (shoulder seal)

Balll IMPROVED MASONS PATENT 1858

Balll MASON

Balll MASON (shoulder seal)

Balll MASON (obverse)
HAHNE & CO., NEWARK, N. J. (base)

Balll MASON IMPROVED (shoulder seal)

Balll MASON IMPROVED (straddle lip top seal)

Balll MASON'S PATENT

Balll MASON PATENT 1858 (shoulder seal)

Balll MASONS PATENT 1858 (shoulder seal)

Balll MASONS PATENT 1858

BBGMCo (monogram, three versions)

Balll STANDARD (wax sealer)

BAMBERGER'S MASON JAR

BAMBERGERS "THE ALWAYS BUSY STORE" NEWARK

CHEF TRADE MARK
        THE BERDAN CO. PAT'D JULY 14, 1908

DECKER'S IOWANA MASON CITY, IOWA

DECKER'S IOWANA MASON CITY, IOWA
            PAT'D JULY 14, 1908

DECKER'S VICTOR MASON CITY, IOWA

Drey IMPROVED EVER SEAL

Drey PERFECT MASON

Drey SQUARE MASON (acquired in Schram purchase)

FAXON BUFFALO NY (base) FAXON BRAND COFFEE
        (circumference of lid) NET 1 LB. (center of lid)

14 OZ. NET FRENCH'S MEDFORD BRAND
                PREPARED MUSTARD

GARDEN WALK ALL PURPOSE MASON JAR BY Ball
            MADE IN U.S.A. (base) (front and back deco-
            rated with Applied Color medallions of fruits and
            vegetables. 1965, made in El Monte, Calif.)

GE GE GE (script)

GENUINE Ball SCULPTURED GLASS (on bottom)
                (beaded seal)

Harvest MASON

Kohrs DAVENPORT, IA. PAT'D JULY 14, 1908

La Abeja (obverse) PAT'D JULY 14, 1908 (reverse)

L & S (base) PAT'D JULY 14, 1908 (lower obverse)

Lustre R. E. TONGUE & BROS. CO. INC. PHILA.
            PAT'D JULY 14, 1908

MASON'S PATENT NOV. 30TH 1858

MASON'S PATENT NOV. 30TH 1858 (obverse)
Balll (reverse)

MASONS PATENT 1858

MC DONALD NEW PERFECT SEAL

MC DONALD PERFECT SEAL

PINT STANDARD (wax sealer)

PORCELAIN BBGMCo (monogram) LINED
QUICK SEAL

QUICK SEAL PAT'D JULY 14, 1908

SAFE SEAL

SAFE SEAL PAT'D JULY 14, 1908

SAMCO GENUINE MASON

SAMCO SUPER MASON (both made for Samuel Mallinger
& Co., Pittsburgh, Pa.)

SELCO SURETY SEAL PAT'D JULY 14, 1908

STANDARD (shepherd's crook under name) (wax sealer)
(acquired with Greenfield purchase)

STRITTMATTER'S PURE HONEY PUT UP BY
F. J. STRITTMATTER & WIFE
R. D. 1 EBENSBURG, PA.

SURE SEAL MADE FOR L. BAMBERGER & CO.

SWAYZEE MASON

SWAYZEE'S FRUIT JAR

SWAYZEE'S IMPROVED MASON

THE BALL JAR (reverse) (Christmas Mason lettering and
style on obverse) (It is highly possible Ball made
all of the so-called Christmas Masons)

The Ball MASON'S IMPROVED PATENT 1858

THE BALL MASON'S N PATENT NOV. 30TH 1858

THE BALL JAR (reverse)
        MASON'S PATENT NOV 30TH 1858 (obverse)

THE BALL MASONS PATENT NOV. 30TH 1858

The Ball PAT APL'D FOR (screw top, shoulder seal)

The Ball PAT. APL'D. FOR. (shoulder seal with metal lid)

The Ball MASON'S PATENT 1858 (obverse)
        IMPROVED (reverse)

The Ball MASON'S PATENT 1858 (PAT. APL'D. FOR.
    ghosted behind MASON'S)

THE HASEROT COMPANY CLEVELAND
        MASON PATENT (shoulder seal)

THE LIQUID The Liquid (in diamond)
        CARBONIC COMPANY (base)
        PAT'D JULY 14, 1908 (lower obverse)

THE RATH PACKING CO. WATERLOO, IOWA.
    PAT'D JULY 14, 1908

TIGHT SEAL PAT'D JULY 14, 1908

TRADEMARK BANNER REGISTERED

TRADEMARK BANNER WARRANTED

TRADEMARK BANNER W M WARRANTED
        TRADEMARK BANNER REG. U.S. PAT.
        OFF. WIDE MOUTH PAT'D JULY 14, 1908

TRADE MARK CLIMAX U.S. PAT OFF REGISTERED
    PAT'D JULY 14, 1908

TROPICAL TF (in diamond shape)
        CANNERS (with three vertical ribs)

VETERAN

WAN-ETA COCOA BOSTON (flint)

WHITNEY MASON PAT'D 1858 (some made for
    Whitney Glass Works, Glassboro, N. J.)

APPENDIX II

Fruit Jar Reference Works

Toulouse, Julian H. *Fruit Jars.*
Thomas Nelson & Sons, Camden, N. J., and Everybodys Press,
Hanover, Pennsylvania, 1969. ($15.00)

Toulouse, Julian H. *Bottle Makers and Their Marks.*
Thomas Nelson Inc., Camden, N. J., 1971. ($15.00).

Roller, Dick *Fruit Jar Newsletter,* Vol. 1, Nos. 1-12.
Dick Roller, Paris, Illinois, 1973-1974. ($5.00).

Creswick, Alice M. *The Red Book of Fruit Jars No. 2.*
Alice M. Creswick, 0-8525 Kenowa SW,
Grand Rapids, Michigan, 1973. ($7.50).

Peters, Frank *Fruit Jar Manual and Price Guide.*
Old Bottle Magazine, Box 243, Bend, Oregon, 1973. ($4.95).

Rodrigues, Arleta *Fruit Jars, Canister to Kerr.*
James Publications, Castro Valley, California, 1973. ($5.00).

AUTHOR'S NOTE:
Julian Toulouse's two books are invaluable references. However, the novice collector should not take every item in these
worthy books as gospel as it applies to fruit jars. Advanced collectors have noted errors in these works.

The Creswick and Peters price guides are both good reference
works and contain the best available pricing information at
this time.

The work of Dick Roller and Mrs. Rodrigues is known to collectors for its careful and painstaking research. Mr. Roller also writes a monthly column on fruit jars in "Old Bottle Magazine" published in Bend, Oregon.

The author, as stated in the preface to this book, will *not* price fruit jars. That is a matter for others better qualified and for the individual buyer and seller to negotiate.

Prices of above works are at time of printing.

APPENDIX III

Ball Glass Manufacturing Plants

(By Date of Construction, Completion or Acquisition)

1882 — Buffalo, N.Y., new plant, burned 1886

1888 — Muncie, Ind., new plant, closed 1962

1898 — Ft. Wayne Glass Works, Upland, Ind.

1901 — Windfall Glass Co., Windfall, Ind.

1904 — Marion Fruit Jar & Bottle Co.,
        Marion, Ind., closed 1910
        Fairmount, Ind., closed 1910
        Converse, Ind., closed 1910
        Coffeyville, Kan., closed 1913

1904 — Port Glass Works, Belleville, Ill., closed 1910

1904 — Loogootee Glass Works, Loogootee, Ind., closed 1906

1904 — Swayzee Glass Co., Swayzee, Ind., closed 1905

1904 — Upland Glass Co., Upland, Ind., closed immediately

1909 — Root Glass Co., Terre Haute, Ind., closed 1913,
          fruit jar plant only.

1909 — Greenfield Fruit Jar & Bottle Co., Greenfield, Ind.,
          purchased on Nov. 20, 1909, sold in 1917

1909 — Mason Fruit Jar & Bottle Co., Coffeyville, Kan.,
          closed 1911

1912 — Premium Glass Co., Coffeyville, Kan., closed 1913
          (acquisition unconfirmed)*

1913 — Texas Bottle Co., Wichita Falls, Tex.

1913 — Wichita Falls, Texas, new plant, closed in 1951,
          sold 1952

1925 — Schram Glass Manufacturing Co., St. Louis, Mo.
          (office only there)
          Plants at: Hillsboro, Ill., sold 1961
                          Huntington, W. Va.,
                              closed before 1941, sold 1944
                          Sapulpa, Okla., closed 1931, sold 1940

1929 — Pine Glass Corp., Okmulgee, Okla., still in operation

1936 — Three Rivers Glass Co., Three Rivers, Tex.,
          closed in 1939 and dismantled, sold 1954

1947 — El Monte, Calif., new plant, still in operation

1948 — Jacksonville, Fla., plant leased from
          Chattanooga Glass Co.

1960 — Asheville, N.C., new plant, still in operation

1961 — Mundelein, Ill., new plant, still in operation

---

*A second glass plant in Coffeyville was purchased by Ball about this time
according to information given the author by Edmund F. Ball, which
was apparently written by Frank C. Ball on Dec. 6, 1921.

INDEX